One **MIRACLE** After Another

One **MIRACLE** After Another

The Pavel Goia Story

GREG BUDD

REVIEW AND HERALD® PUBLISHING ASSOCIATION
Since 1861 | www.reviewandherald.com

This book was
Edited by Steven S. Winn
Copyedited by James Cavil
Cover design by Trent Truman
Cover image of water droplets: © iStockphoto.com / Sergey Peterman
Cover image of Pavel Goia: Supplied
Interior design by Heather Rogers
Interior image of water: © iStockphoto.com / Airyelf
Typeset: Bembo 11/13

Printed by Pacific Press® Publishing Association.
Printed in U.S.A.

Additional copies of this book can be purchased by calling toll-free 1-800-765-6955 or by visiting http://www.adventistbookcenter.com.

Library of Congress Cataloging-in-Publication Data
Budd, Greg, 1954- .
One miracle after another : the Pavel Goia story / Greg Budd.
p. cm.
1. Goia, Pavel. 2. Seventh-day Adventists—Romania—Clergy—Biography. 3. Seventh-day Adventists—United States—Clergy—Biography. I. Title.
BX6193.G55B93 2009
286.7092—dc22
[B]

2009030549

ISBN 978-0-8280-2496-9

January 2019

I dedicate this book
to those who courageously stand
for faith though fiercely opposed
by corrupt political and religious systems.

Many around the world are enduring persecution,
imprisonment, starvation, and death for their faith
at this very moment. It is my desire that you will be reminded
to lift them up in prayer as you read the pages that follow.
In the near future many more will be opposed by these
same corrupt forces as the spiritual battle comes to a climax
on planet earth. If you are called upon to stand for your faith,
I pray the stories in this book will serve as
powerful reminders of God's faithfulness.

This exciting, well-written book will stretch your faith and encourage you to trust and to know God more intimately. Pavel's faith in a big God inspires us to believe, to trust, to pray, to expect, and to receive.

—Ruthie Jacobsen
North American Division Prayer Ministries

Pavel Goia's experiences as an Adventist Christian in communist Romania are truly remarkable. This book shows that God is present to help His people when they put themselves on the line for Him. We in the West are used to freedom and practicing our faith without great conflict. We need to read stories like this to help prepare ourselves for more challenging times that prophecy says are ahead. I recommend this book to all those who want a more dynamic faith experience with God.

—Donald W. Corkum, President
Wisconsin Conference of Seventh-day Adventists

This book is filled with wonderful stories of how God came into the life of a young man growing up during the difficult and perilous times of Communist Romania and how specifically and personally God spoke with Pavel all along the way. It is truly inspirational from the beginning to the end.

—Ralph Hendershot

As a student of mine, it did not take me long to realize that Paul Goia was a man led by God. This book is amazing in how God leads and answers prayer.

—Jack J. Blanco, Professor Emeritus
Southern Adventist University

While reading Pavel Goia's manuscript, I was repeatedly moved to tears at the incredible stories of God's intervention in answer to Pavel's prayers. I was also deeply moved to re-dedicate my own life in faithfulness to God and willingness to trust Him come what may, as Pavel did. As I write these lines, I am teaching classes at the Romanian Adventist Seminary, just a few miles from where many of the stories in this book took place. The realization of such mighty miracles that God performed in Romania during the days of Communist persecution and trial has made my travels in this country feel like I am treading on holy ground! I recommend this book to all who wish to have their faith strengthened in the prayer-answering God who still works powerful miracles like in biblical times.

—Richard Davidson, Chair
Old Testament Department, Andrews University Theological Seminary

The marvelous experiences by Pastor Goia are the stuff you read from the book of Acts: miracles, faithfulness, amazing intercessions by the God of heaven. All this was possible because one man chose everyday to belong to God and God alone. Nothing is impossible for God, and that extends for those who serve Him fully. This book will make you want to drop to your knees and fully surrender to a Lord who longs to work marvelous works among His children.

—Ron Clouzet, Director
North American Division Evangelism Institute

Contents

CHAPTER 1:

Say Not, I Am a Child

I don't believe there is a God!" Pavel Goia blurted into the darkness. "I'm tired of the whole foolish notion. I feel as if I'm going crazy! How could I have allowed myself to be duped? Believing in a Being who doesn't even exist has stolen all the fun from my life. My friends are out having the time of their lives while I lie here feeling lost and condemned. How many more nights do I need to toss and turn without sleep? I hate listening to the seconds ticking endlessly away. Lying here with thoughts of guilt echoing and reechoing through my mind feels like a nightmare. I would give anything to silence that haunting Voice: "Pavel, if you die tonight, you'll be lost forever!"

One thought after another bombarded the troubled young man attempting to escape the torture of his soul. Poor Pavel—he had no place to run and nowhere to hide. But he had made up his mind to bring his misery to an end. "I have to put these crazy ideas about God behind me and just enjoy life the way all my friends do," Pavel said half aloud as he pulled the covers aside.

"That does it. I'm going to town to have some fun—I can't sleep anyway," he muttered under his breath as he scanned the room for his pants.

Attempting to find his clothes in the shadows of a darkened room was not an easy task, but with a little persistence he succeeded. Carefully calculating his escape, he tiptoed from room to room so as not to awaken his parents. But when he reached the living room, he stopped in his tracks. The moonlight shining through the window outlined the silhouette of his father kneeling in prayer. Pavel had often happened upon his father in prayer, but why tonight? His praying father was the last thing his troubled mind desired to see as he made his escape from home and his parents' God.

His pace quickened as he stepped out into the darkness. From the dim lights lining the street, he glanced in the direction of shadowy objects stretching out before him. The haunting image of his father praying followed him from shadow to shadow as he hurried to the city and his waiting friends.

"Hey, Pavel! Glad you could make it!" called one of his friends with a bit of a slur as he approached their usual hangout.

One of the central parks known as the Little Market had become a favorite spot for his friends to pass the evening hours drinking and smoking. It was also an ideal spot to watch for a young woman to happen along. Many factory workers had to walk by this strategic location on their way home from work as the second shift ended. Whenever the young men were fortunate enough for it to be a woman, she instantly became the center of attention. A fanfare of loud whistling greeted each approaching prospect, and a barrage of suggestive invitations followed as she passed in front of them. The routine was nearly the same each time. The young partyers enthusiastically continued their little charade until it became clear that their subject had not been duly impressed by their antics.

"We've been having a real good time," chimed in another. His claim was quickly validated by a concert of loud, drunken laughter. In the dim light Pavel could see the evidence on all sides. The "market crowd" had obviously arrived much earlier than he had. With piles of cigarette butts strewn carelessly about and nearly empty bottles dangling in hand, it was not difficult to see that a valiant attempt to have a "good time" was in progress.

"Pavel, how about one of your jokes? Have you got one for us tonight?" called out a familiar voice. Within a few moments Pavel was the center of attention as he recited a favorite from his repertoire of off-color jokes. He was in his element as the entertainer.

No one offered him anything to drink or smoke since he had never desired to join them in their vices. But he sure knew how to make them laugh. Pavel knew more dirty jokes than the rest of them put together. However, he really didn't fit with this rough and rowdy bunch, even though he had been spending a lot of time with them. Many of them had shown little interest in school, and nearly all came from homes lacking in moral support.

In contrast, Pavel was from a third-generation Christian family and made almost perfect grades in all his classes. Often he felt like a misfit in this group of young men aimlessly adrift. They lived from one "good time" to the next. No one seemed to mind that Pavel was a little different; his quick wit and ability to tell stories kept them laughing for hours night after night.

Once again he had his audience smiling and laughing with his evening entertainment. "Hey, look over there at that babe headed our way," interrupted someone from Pavel's intoxicated audience. The unexpected approach of a young woman in their direction created an instant distraction. Now she had the undivided attention of his audience. Lewd and obscene suggestions accompanied by loud whistling ensued as the unsuspecting young woman approached.

As she attempted to pass the inebriated young men, several of them quickly surrounded her. Frantically her wide eyes searched for an escape, but she was completely blocked in. Terrified, she pleaded with them to let her go, but it was no use. Pavel watched in horror as his friends began to taunt her with some very suggestive and inappropriate gestures; they seemed to have lost their minds. After a moment or two he could endure no more of their outrageous behavior. Facing her captors, Pavel yelled, "Let her go!"

The smiles that had recently covered their faces as they listened to his stories and jokes dissolved into angry looks and sneers of disgust as Pavel earnestly protested their behavior. "Come on, you guys, let her go! What you're doing is wrong," Pavel pleaded with all the boldness he could muster.

His attempted defense temporarily shifted their attention from the captive young woman to her defender. Angrily one of the leaders lashed back, "Who do you think you are, telling us what's right and wrong? I don't remember anyone inviting you to tell us what to do!"

Repulsed by their behavior, Pavel stepped back. Wanting no part of their passion-driven madness, he wished only for a way to assist the sobbing young woman pleading to go free. Realizing he was equally helpless, he continued his retreat.

"Get out of here and don't come back," they sneered. It was clear that they were not about to be swayed from their intentions. A sick feeling filled his stomach as he turned to walk away from the drunken, cursing "market crowd." Were these the same guys he thought were his friends just a few moments earlier? Nothing about them felt very appealing now. This night had gone anything but the way he had hoped it would.

Pavel's attempt to run from his guilty conscience to his friends in town had not quieted his troubled thoughts or given him the peace he was so desperately seeking. His journey home was more miserable than his escape had been.

The rest of the night was anything but peaceful; once he was in bed, it was only more tossing and turning. Adding to the pangs of his guilty conscience were the fresh images of the horror-stricken eyes and the sobbing voice of the young woman pleading to be set free.

He began the next day tortured by turbulent emotions. Scenes from the night before refused to leave him, and now he felt worse than ever. Before long the scenes that troubled him became the passionate disgust of the neighborhood as news of the previous night spread from neighbor to neighbor. "Have you heard about the young men in town last night who violently abused one of our innocent young girls? The police have every one of them in custody. I hope none of them ever sees the light of day again. If they throw away the prison keys, it would be too good for those worthless bums."

As Pavel learned the fate of the girl he was horrified. The sick feeling he had experienced the night before instantly returned. Those he had thought were his friends would no doubt spend many long years in prison. But he had been spared. In reality he knew he could easily have been sitting in jail at this very moment waiting for a trial if he had not walked away when he did.

He began to feel extremely grateful for the rejection he had experienced from the market crowd. Imagining the terrified young woman pleading for her freedom removed any lingering sympathy he may have had for those he thought were his friends. The image of his praying father returned as he contemplated his narrow escape from a lengthy prison sentence.

With sleep escaping him once again, he lay thoughtfully looking at the same shadows on the ceiling he had stared at the night before. However, this night was very different from his recent ones filled with anxious, guilt-ridden thoughts. This one would be spent not running from God but *to* Him. In the stillness of the night Pavel's mind began to retrace the earlier years of his life.

Growing up in a Christian family in Communist Romania had not been easy. Christianity was viewed as a crutch for the weak and simple. Attending church was openly ridiculed, and Bibles were forbidden. For those who insisted on embracing faith, limited employment opportunities were just one of the consequences that could be expected. Many times his family had endured extremely difficult consequences resulting from their faithfulness to God.

As Pavel replayed the many challenges his family had faced, he couldn't help feeling grateful for the strong Christian heritage his grandfather had passed along. Feelings of thankfulness replaced the resentful, bitter sentiments of the night before. What a different perspective just one night had made.

He now understood his praying father, kneeling night after night, to be the only difference between himself and his companions incarcerated in concrete cells. They no doubt would experience some sleepless nights of their own.

Pavel couldn't help smiling as memories of his early childhood came vividly back to mind. Growing up in Turnu Severin in the southwestern part of Romania along the Danube River had provided him a vast countryside to explore, and the river had many wonderful places for him and his sisters to swim during the hot summer months. Ancient Roman ruins not far from his home also became a favorite place for exploring. Only the imagination of a young boy could rightly bring back to life all the history that had been resting in silence for countless centuries.

Fond memories of his church and the love they had shown him came flooding back as his sleepless night continued. As a very young boy he had been gifted with an exceptionally sharp memory. Reciting memorized Scripture passages to the church members was something he looked forward to each week. The older members especially anticipated his oratories. He had come to love the praise and attention following each of his perfect performances. The rewards were not only flowery compliments but often candy and other treasures known to be appreciated by children. The numerous rewards provided him strong motivation to enhance his performances, and in a short time he was reciting entire chapters from the Bible, much to the delight of the congregation. Enjoying the special attention from his admirers, he added singing special music to his ecclesiastical repertoire.

Singing had been part of his family worship experience for as long as he could remember. With a gifted voice and a sharp memory, learning songs to sing at church came easily. Many well-meaning members had no doubt been too free with their compliments, praises, and gifts, and very early in life he came to view himself as a spiritually superior Christian.

The hairstyles for boys began to change, but not Pavel's. To add further to his image of the "good boy at church," he faithfully went to the barbershop every two weeks. As his childhood memories replayed in his mind, he had to admit, I could well have been one of the world's youngest Pharisees. He was a "good boy," and he knew it.

As he lay staring up into the darkness his life journey continued. One of his most memorable moments had taken place when he was just 5. A visiting pastor had come as a guest speaker for a special service at the church. Many times he had recalled portions of this service. Looking into the faces of the congregation, the visiting pastor had introduced his message: "My passage for this evening is taken from Jeremiah 29:11." Taking his Bible, he invited them to read the passage aloud:

"'I know the plans that I have for you,' declares the Lord, 'plans for welfare and not for calamity to give you a future and a hope'" (NASB).

Pavel had listened intently as the pastor carefully explained the passage. "It doesn't matter how young or old you are or what your present circumstances might be. God has a plan for you."

As the message continued little Pavel had tried to comprehend how this could include a 5-year-old. It wasn't hard to believe that God had a plan for his grandfather, for he had faithfully followed Him all his life. Looking at his father and mother, he could see how God might have a plan for their lives, too—but a 5-year-old? It seemed as if this might be more than the passage had intended.

At the conclusion of the message it was clear that the congregation had been blessed and inspired with a wonderful, fresh picture of a personal God. One by one the members filed by the pastor, thanking him for his message as they exited the church. At last it was his opportunity to address the speaker. Standing directly in front of the pastor, he looked up into his eyes and asked with all the earnestness he possessed, "Does God really have a plan for me, or am I too young?" With a big smile he was assured that God's plans included even someone 5 years old.

"Have you ever prayed and asked God if He has a plan for you?" inquired the pastor.

"No, I guess I haven't," he had replied thoughtfully as he walked toward the door.

Deeply pondering the pastor's challenge, he had made his way out to the big apple tree in the churchyard. He had played many times under this tree, but today was different. He had come to ask God a very important question.

Closing his eyes, he began to pour out his heart. "Dear God, I am just a little boy 5 years old. Do you really have a plan for me, too?" For several minutes he continued to pour out his heart in prayer. If God had a plan for his life, he wanted to know about it.

When he felt he had sufficiently presented his case, he waited anxiously for a voice from heaven to make known the plan. What would God say to him? Quietly he waited for a voice from above, but only the sound of the rustling leaves broke the silence.

Disappointed but not discouraged, he thought of another approach. Spotting his father with his Bible standing and talking to another member in front of the church, he quickly made his way to his side. Looking up into his face, he said, "I just prayed and asked God if He had a plan for me, but He didn't say anything." A broad smile came to the faces of the men listening to Pavel's plight.

Without waiting for either of them to speak, he took his father's Bible from his hands. Holding the sacred book, he pondered how he might discover God's plan for his life from the verses within. Randomly he parted the pages and put his finger on a verse. Surely God would outline the plan for his life from His Word. Looking again into his father's face, he asked, "Would you please read this verse?"

Slowly removing his finger from Jeremiah 1:5, his father began to scan the verse. His broad smile quickly faded as he realized the significance of the passage beneath his son's finger. In a very thoughtful voice he began to read:

"Before I formed thee in the belly I knew thee; and before thou camest forth out of the womb I sanctified thee, and I ordained thee a prophet unto the nations. Then said I, Ah, Lord God! behold, I cannot speak: for I am a child. But the Lord said unto me, Say not, I am a child: for thou shalt go to all that I shall send thee, and whatsoever I command thee thou shalt speak" (verses 5-7).

As Pavel lay on his bed reliving the moment, a smile came to his face. He felt the excitement all over again.

For the next several minutes he had jumped for joy telling everyone that he was going to speak for God. He freely informed the church members lingering in conversation, "I am going to be a pastor or a missionary." He was going to speak for God. God had made it clear, with the words "Say not, I am a child," that he wasn't too young to have a plan for his life. He had been chosen to be God's special spokesman.

On the spot he embraced his commission as God's messenger. Diligently ever after he would evaluate each individual to determine his spiritual condition and subsequent needs. For those falling short (in his estimation as a pastor-evangelist), he would enlighten them. Each person he deemed in need of repentance would receive a heartfelt appeal. He would warn the world of its fate without God.

Shortly after beginning the first grade Pavel shifted his evangelistic focus to his classmates. It didn't take him long to complete his assessment of their needs. In his estimation as an evangelist his entire class was found wanting, with the exception of himself, of course. What an opportunity for his first major evangelistic campaign!

Marching to the front of the class in bold preacherlike style, he began his discourse to the 45 students. "You must all begin attending church, or you will surely burn in hell!" His presentation had been brief, but the content had remained focused through to the end. He was convinced he had provided just the spiritual enlightenment for which his classmates had been longing.

What could have gone wrong? Pavel had wondered as he stared out the window. It was time to leave for church, and not a single classmate stood waiting in front of his house. The long line of imagined waiting classmates had not materialized. Not a single convert had emerged as the result of his first sermon.

Disappointed but certainly not diverted from his course, Pavel began to strategize for his next presentation. Perhaps the impending penalty had not been adequately emphasized. Next time he would make certain he did not gloss over the punishment.

After a few days he felt that the time had come to repeat his sermon. At the conclusion of his second presentation he felt assured his point could not have been missed or taken lightly. To his amazement, the sentiment of his classmates remained unchanged. Several times he made his way to the front of the classroom to remind his classmates they would soon suffer eternal punishment if they did not follow his example. After several such sermons Pavel decided to change his strategy. If fear couldn't persuade them, maybe a reward-based tactic would achieve his goal.

Standing before his classmates once again, Pavel began his final appeal. "I would like to share with you the secret to my unrivaled popularity. The reason I am the 'coolest' one in school is that I go to church. If you want to be really 'cool' like me, you need to come to church too."

The next week, to the amazement of the congregation, Pavel led his entire class down the aisle to the front of the church in search of the promised reward. However, each of them returned home having discovered no greater "coolness" than before the service. Consequently the attendance of his guests abruptly ended after their first visit, in spite of the enlightenment he had provided them. Evidently they had missed the truth that multiple visits were required to produce all they beheld in him. What was wrong with them? Pavel wondered. Without a doubt they had been blinded as to who they really were. If they weren't ready to become "cool" yet, perhaps he should begin by helping them with some character development. It was all becoming clear to him now—their problem was humility!

Pavel could not help smiling as he thought of his former zeal as a pastor-evangelist. He had put his whole heart into his calling, only to discover it was more difficult than he had first realized.

Alone in the darkness he pondered the changes that had slowly transpired in his life. Gradually the focus of his personal invitation from God had faded. For the past several years he had gone to church just to please his father. More and more he had sought the approval of his friends in place of God's. Staying out until 2:00 or 3:00 in the morning with his friends had definitely contributed to the deterioration of his faith. Many times he had heard God's voice remind him of his special prayer under the apple tree and the answer that had come from his father's Bible. But repeatedly he ignored the still small voice inviting him to return to a life of peace and happiness.

Feelings of sorrow and regret now swept over him as he thought of the choices he had made over the past few years. Pulling back the covers, he slipped to his knees beside the bed. Opening his heart to God, he began to pray, "Lord, if You're not too angry with me, and if You still want me, I want to come back to You. If that was really You speaking to me in front of the church when I was 5, I want to accept Your invitation. I don't know how You can forgive someone like me. Can You possibly accept me after all the times I've denied You? Is there still a way?"

Lying prostrate on the floor, he continued to pour out his heart to God hour after hour. At 5:00 in the morning a wonderful peace and acceptance filled his whole being.

Opening his Bible, he prayed, "Lord, please speak to me from Your Word once again." As he randomly parted the pages, his Bible fell open to Isaiah 54:8-10:

"In a little wrath I hid my face from thee for a moment; but with everlasting kindness will I have mercy on thee, saith the Lord thy Redeemer. For this is as the waters of Noah unto me: for as I have sworn that the waters of Noah should no more go over the earth; so have I sworn that I would not be wroth with thee, nor rebuke thee. For the mountains shall depart, and the hills be removed; but my kindness shall not depart from thee, neither shall the covenant of my peace be removed, saith the Lord that hath mercy on thee."

Tears of joy filled his eyes as the living Word sank deep into his heart. With the assurance of acceptance and the weight of his sin removed, he thanked God and solemnly covenanted with Him, "I'm never going to leave my place of prayer and worship in the morning for any reason from now on, until I know for sure that You are with me."

Pavel's heart overflowed as he walked from his bedroom to awaken his parents so they could share in the joy of his renewed commitment to God. Once again he found his father on his knees. As his father stood to greet him, he earnestly pleaded, "Please—keep praying for me. I've been struggling for a long time, but tonight I've given my heart to God."

Looking him in the eye, his father informed him, "Every time you saw me praying, it was for you. I know what it feels like to struggle. I struggled too as a young man, but in the midst of my troubles God gave me a verse in Scripture that felt as though it was all mine. Listen to the words that God spoke to me when I was young:

"He will turn again, he will have compassion upon us; he will subdue our iniquities; and thou wilt cast all their sins into the depths of the sea" (Micah 7:19).

With a smile his father challenged, "Perhaps God will give you a verse someday as well."

"He already has," Pavel said with a broad smile. The pillow that had shared his many sleepless nights invited him back to bed. Resting in the first real peace he had experienced in years, he closed his eyes and slept. How sweet it was!

CHAPTER 2:

I Will Take Care of You

Before the first rays of dawn peeked through his bedroom window Pavel slipped from beneath the covers to his knees beside the bed. He was determined to keep the promise he had made the night before. *Will God be waiting? Will He speak to me again today?* he wondered as he bowed his head.

"Father, it's me, Pavel. I'm here, just as I promised. Please help me to be a true friend to You. I am so thankful that You still want me. Please change my heart. Make me over again the way You have been wanting to," he prayed softly.

A feeling of God's presence began to settle in around him just as he had experienced the night before. How grateful he was that God had not abandoned him in his rebellion. With a smile he reached for his Bible. How he hoped the words would come alive again, and to his amazement, it felt as if each word had been written just for him.

As new spiritual insights illuminated his mind he looked up, praying, "Father, You are so wonderful. You are beyond comprehension." He never dreamed that the Creator of the vast universe would speak so personally to someone as undeserving as he. His heart was overflowing in an atmosphere of grace. The assurance that God would go with him throughout the day came to him just it had the night before. As his morning appointment with God came to an end Pavel could feel a broad smile across his face.

What a wonderful way to begin the day! he thought, comparing this morning with so many others of the past few years. His new friendship with God had blessed him in ways he never could have imagined.

As Pavel reveled in the blessings of his time with God, memories of the chaos that had grown out of his teenage attempts for freedom came back to him. Scene after scene replayed in his mind. Television and movies had occupied most of his spare time—as well as the time he really didn't have to spare. Long into the night he would watch one movie after another. They had become his routine rather than occasional entertainment.

Exhausted and bleary-eyed the morning after his movie marathons, he would scramble out of bed at 7:45. With school starting at 8:00, he faced the ever-present problem that it took 20 minutes to walk to school. A mad frenzy characterized his search for something to put on each morning. It was a race against the clock, and his bedroom was the racetrack. Not every hair was in perfect order as he exited the front door trying to run and tie his shoe at the same time.

Nearly the same time each day Pavel made his grand entrance into the classroom—always 10 to 15 minutes into the period, with the teacher having already begun the instruction. One morning he had come up with an ingenious, foolproof excuse for his tardiness that he was sure even the brightest professors would be unable to see through.

Rushing into the classroom with the lecture already in progress, he began his speech. "Early this morning I started out for school in order to be one of the first to arrive. With the extra time I allowed for the busy traffic, I was sure I would be early. Everything was fine until I came to Central Boulevard. I had no way of knowing that a funeral procession would be passing at the very instant I needed to cross the street. The procession must have been for a government dignitary of some kind, because the line of cars stretched as far as I could see. I waited and waited for them to pass. The procession was barely creeping—it moved only half as fast as most funerals. It seemed as if it would never end. I realized after 15 or 20 minutes that I would probably be a little late as only half the cars had passed. I would have made a mad dash through the procession, but out of respect I decided to wait patiently. Just as soon as the last car passed by, I hurried here as fast as I could."

Concluding his dramatic presentation, he walked back to take his seat. He was sure he had been convincing enough that even the most intuitive had been swept away by his eloquence.

The next morning he reasoned that since everything had gone so smoothly, why not use the same foolproof alibi again? A new funeral procession arrived at Central Boulevard each day at precisely the moment he was about to cross. After numerous dramatic oratories, the teacher came up with a time-saving alternative to his presentation. As Pavel came through the door he would simply ask, without looking up,

"Goia, another funeral?" Pavel needed only to nod in agreement and walk to his seat. His plan turned out to be even more ingenious than he first imagined! Now a simple yes or a nod was all it took to fool his entire classroom completely. Pavel may not have thoroughly considered one factor, however. He had been responsible for burying many more dignitaries than existed in the entire country! From where were all these important people coming? And how unfortunate that so many should die in succession!

As his recent past replayed in his mind a new sense of gratitude emerged. His past had been nothing short of chaotic! The biggest shock of all came the first day he really did arrive at school early. The entire class stared in disbelief. How thankful the undertaker must have been for a little reprieve.

With each passing day Pavel's love affair with God deepened. The Bible promises he had learned as a child came flooding back through his mind. Now they weren't just beautiful words—he could claim them as his own promises. Opening his heart to God in prayer had become like talking to his Best Friend. Each morning he opened his eyes with a sense of expectation and an eagerness for what the day would bring. He could hardly wait to discover the new blessing that awaited him. The Bible became a book alive with power. Over and over he experienced the morning's Scripture supply him with just the strength he needed for the day. Encountering the words of Jeremiah in Lamentations 3:22, 23, he could only look heavenward and say, "Lord, Your Word is true. This is what You do for me each day."

"The Lord's lovingkindnesses indeed never cease, for His compassions never fail. They are new every morning; great is Your faithfulness" (NASB).

Often, as God spoke personally to him, tears would well up in his eyes. "Lord, how could I have missed all this before?" he whispered. It was one thing to read the words of Isaiah 50—it was altogether another to experience them:

"He awakens Me morning by morning, He awakens My ear to listen as a disciple" (verse 4, NASB).

"Thank You, Lord that I didn't need my alarm clock to wake me up this morning. You are faithful, just as Your Word says. The first thoughts to greet me each morning are Your words. It's thrilling to hear You call my name and whisper, 'I've been waiting for you.' Your loving-kindness is truly beyond comprehension," Pavel prayed as he reflected on the excitement he was experiencing in his newfound friendship with God.

He knew that without God's help, his desire to be "cool" would regain control in his life. Seeking his friends' acceptance had taken him far from God once, and he determined by His grace not ever to let pride rule his life again. Openly in prayer he confessed his weakness before leaving his house each day. He prayed that God would help him care more about what He thought than what others thought.

A remarkable transformation began to take place. Thinking about and talking to God each morning began to make him more like his new Friend. Things he had been struggling with began to lose their appeal. The desire was just gone. God was changing him, just as He had promised.

Growing up with the image of his father kneeling in prayer had continually perplexed him—until a few days ago. Why anyone would spend so much time talking to a God he couldn't see or hear had been a total mystery. But now he understood perfectly.

The example of Jesus in the Gospel of Mark became his pattern for each new day:

"Rising up a great while before day, he went out, and departed into a solitary place, and there prayed" (Mark 1:35).

He resolved to make the secret place of prayer that empowered Jesus' life his own. What an experience! Life had taken on a whole new meaning. With the psalmist he could say:

"All my springs of joy are in you" (Psalm 87:7, NASB).

A test of loyalty came a few weeks after promising God that he would never leave home without knowing He was with him. After inviting God to awaken him for their time together, he had awakened between 4:00 and 5:00 a.m., but for some reason had fallen back asleep. When his eyes focused on the alarm clock, he groaned—it was 7:30.

"How could this have happened?" Pavel wondered. Now what should he do? He had to decide whether to stay for his appointment with God or make a mad dash for the classroom. A real struggle began. His class schedule had changed. In place of the teacher familiar with funerals, he had the most hard-nosed Communist teacher in the school. Everyone feared him. He made sure everyone understood that it wouldn't be wise to cross him. Even worse, he openly mocked the idea of God. To be late to one of his classes wouldn't soon be forgotten. Pictures of facing his displeasure began to taunt him. A voice began urging him to forget his promise just this once. After all, God certainly wanted him to be a good student.

What should he do?

Another voice began to speak quietly to him: "Are you going to trust Me and spend the time it takes to know I am with you? I have gone ahead of you solving problems and working out difficulties. Will you trust Me with this one, too?" He knew there really was only one choice he could make and be true to his agreement. Quietly he began his time with God.

From time to time pictures of a furious professor flashed before him, and each time he surrendered them to God. It was almost two hours before he felt the peace and assurance he needed.

Pavel prayed each step of the longest walk he had ever taken to school. What would happen? Would he be expelled from his first-period class? He knew it was a required class to graduate. With each thought challenging his peace, he simply said, "God, I'm giving it to You."

It was almost 10:00 when he came walking into class. He had completely missed his first class, and second period was in session.

Taking his seat, he looked over at a friend in the next row. His glance was returned with a look of astonishment. Leaning over a bit, his friend whispered, "How did you know the professor in first period would be sick today? Your timing is amazing! And that's not all. This teacher somehow forgot to take attendance. Can you believe it? That's never happened before. Goia, you have got to be the luckiest guy on earth!"

Pavel sighed with relief as he realized that God had blessed him for remaining faithful to Him. Over and over he watched little details work out in ways he could never have solved on his own.

God's blessings followed him not only in the classroom but also in his work. Since he had given his life to God, he had a growing desire to excel as a craftsman. His father's excellent reputation as a contractor had people willing to wait for his skill and expertise for their projects. In his after-school hours the family business provided Pavel the opportunity to learn various aspects of building as well as to earn some spending money.

Of all the skills he learned, cutting glass was one of his favorites. God soon blessed him with proficiency and accuracy that few craftsmen ever acquire. Several commercial projects required fire-rated wire glass to be used in specified locations. Even fewer tradesmen had experience cutting this special glass. With his father as his tutor he learned the trade secrets of this special skill.

Shortly after Pavel turned 16 the opportunity came to prove that he was indeed a competent craftsman, not just a punk teenager in the workplace. The county building commissioner had come to rely on Pavel's father to help him out when he was falling behind on completion deadlines. Often unforeseen problems would arise, causing costly delays. Many times it appeared that the project could never be finished on time. Frantically the commissioner would contact Mr. Goia to help him meet a deadline. Over and over God had blessed, enabling him to accomplish far more than anyone thought possible. It was always a sore spot, however, when the weekend came and Mr. Goia announced he would not be coming to work the next day, as it was his day of worship. Repeatedly the plea would come for him to work, but he always remained faithful to his convictions.

Once again the county building commissioner was in a jam. One of the country's largest auto repair centers was under construction. It would be a state-of-the-art building with multilevel parking alongside. The project was scheduled to be completed by the end of October, and it had fallen significantly behind. To make matters worse, the president of the country was scheduled to visit the city at the end of October. Seeing this architectural masterpiece was on his agenda.

One of the areas that had fallen critically behind was the cutting of wire glass. Several areas required this special glass to meet code. He had searched everywhere, but few people had the knowledge and skill to cut this kind of glass. Mr. Goia just happened to be one of those few who could help him out. Desperately he pleaded for another rescue from Mr. Goia.

"I'm so sorry I can't help you. I am scheduled solid until January with deadlines of my own," replied Mr. Goia apologetically. "But I know someone who could do it for you. My son has become very skilled at cutting wire glass. He can cut it as well as I can. I'm sure he would be glad to help you out," he offered. The commissioner was not excited about hiring a 16-year-old for such a difficult assignment, but with two months of work needing to be finished in less than a month, what choice did he have?

Pavel was excited to be able to prove himself as a craftsman. How thankful he was for the confidence his new life had given him. As soon as school was out he went directly to the construction site. Finding the chief engineer, he introduced himself as the glass cutter who had been hired by the building commissioner. The haughty chief engineer was not pleased, and an angry scowl instantly darkened his face. He grumbled that he had been "sent a kid" rather than a man. He needed a specialist—not some teenager still wet behind the ears. He had enough problems without having to babysit.

In spite of his new cursing supervisor Pavel cheerfully went to work. Each time he used his diamond scoring tool a perfect cut followed. The installation went just as smoothly. He could never remember a time his work had been performed with such proficiency. With his putty knife in one hand and a bead of glazing in the other he formed perfectly symmetrical glazing around the edges of the glass. He was amazed as each opening was perfectly completed and in record time. Late each night he worked attempting to meet the deadline.

When the first weekend came, Pavel announced he would not be at work the next day, as he was a Christian and it was his day of worship. A fit of cursing such as he had never heard began to spew out of the engineer's mouth. The outraged supervisor made it quite clear he despised having him on the project. He had been sure Pavel couldn't do the work, and when Pavel had proved he could do it perfectly and in record time, the supervisor hated him all the more. There was no way to please the man. In spite of all the threats and insults Pavel was in church the following day.

When Pavel returned to the job site, he was insulted in every way possible. It was clear that his supervisor was determined to make his life as miserable as he could. He didn't want a kid on his job, and the fact that Pavel was a Christian made it all the worse. Pavel couldn't even walk from one place to the other on the job site without enduring profane cursing and gesturing. Patiently he did his job, enduring the daily abusive onslaught.

At last the project was finished. He was exhausted, but he was proud of both the quality and record speed in which his work had been accomplished.

Each classification of work had a posted pay schedule. Some work was scheduled for hourly compensation. Other workers were paid a set amount for each item completed. The glass work had a pay schedule for each square meter of installed glass. As he completed each opening Pavel kept a running tally of his square meters. He was making far more than the men around him. The tradesmen earned 1,600 to 1,800 lei per month working at an hourly rate. The project supervisor, who despised him, was earning 2,400 lei per month. In the three weeks he had worked with the wire glass by the square meter he had earned 5,500 lei.

Two months and two men had been allotted for his part of the project. With God working as his partner he completed it in just three weeks. There was a song in his heart as he left the job site.

But the song quickly faded as he went to collect his pay. The supervisor's face twisted in a fit of rage with more cursing as he screamed, "I don't even make that much money, and I'm the chief engineer! I'm not about to pay some punk kid twice as much as I make. I am going to pay you 1,200 lei and not any more!" Pavel protested, referring to the posted pay schedule, but to no avail.

Sadly he made his way home. Was this the way he was to be repaid for all the long hours he had worked? It wasn't fair, and he wasn't going to settle for it without a protest. The county building commissioner had been the one to hire him, and to the county building commissioner he would appeal. Walking into the City-County Building felt somewhat intimidating. Who would listen to a young boy's protest against a project engineer?

The secretary for the county building engineer's department listened to his plea for justice. "You come back in the morning at 8:00 sharp, and I'll give you the first five minutes on the schedule," she promised. With a smile Pavel thanked her, realizing his invisible Partner was still working for him.

With a start he sat up in bed. It was 7:45 a.m. "Oh no, I've overslept again," he moaned. He was supposed to be at the City-County Building in just 15 minutes. Grabbing his clothes, he started for the door. With his hand on the doorknob, he heard a voice say, "Pavel, did you pray? Are you going to leave home without Me today?"

"But I have an appointment with the commissioner. What will he think of me if I don't even show up?" Pavel reasoned.

"Are you going to trust Me this time, or are you going on your own today?" replied the still small voice.

Choosing to trust God come what may, he decided not to leave until he knew God was with him. It was 10:00 when that familiar peace returned to his heart. Looking at the clock he thought about just canceling the trip to town. But after a few moments he asked himself, "What do I have to lose? I might as well go and see what happens."

The same polite smile greeted him as he approached the secretary's desk to apologize for his tardiness. She assured him that he shouldn't worry, as the prime minister had come and had been in meetings all morning with each of the department heads.

"You come back tomorrow, and I'll see what I can do," she said. Relieved, Pavel turned to leave. Just as he reached the door she called to him, "Wait."

At that very minute the building commissioner opened the door of the conference room and started across the hall for the restroom. He came over to her desk to see what all the excitement was about. After listening for a moment, he told the secretary to validate Pavel's story from the job site and prepare a full report for him to review.

The next day Pavel received a phone call from the secretary. "You can come down and pick up your check." With a three-month paycheck in his pocket Pavel walked home with a spring in his step.

CHAPTER 3:

Glass Trouble

I *think I could go into business for myself,* Pavel thought as he walked home from the building commissioner's office. *I could make some real money if I kept working with glass.* The money he had earned from the commercial construction project was just the inspiration he needed to pursue a business of his own. A little simple math promised him more spending money than most tradesmen earned to support their families.

He knew the government controlled all enterprise. Only those registering under the category Mandatory Private could operate a personal business. Audits were performed on a regular basis to ensure business owners remained in compliance. The system was quite simple: the business owner was allowed to keep 35 percent of the profit while 65 percent went directly to the government. No one argued; it was just the way it was.

Upon obtaining his permit, he rented a room adjoining another business. The location was ideal. His storefront was on a main street near the downtown area. With the purchase of a few tools he was ready for business.

The large government cooperative located at the center of each city and town regulated the sale of all building materials. The co-op consisted of a complex of large warehouses. A separate building housed the materials for each trade. Locating the glass division of the local co-op, Pavel filled out the necessary paperwork to purchase glass on consignment, allowing him to pay only for the materials he used. The large warehouse was stocked with wooden crates containing glass of all sizes and thicknesses. One area displayed decorative specialty glasses, such as frosted, beveled, and wire glass.

Pavel selected two crates of the most commonly sized glass as stock for his new shop. The crates housed 22 sheets of glass measuring six feet by seven feet. With glass and crating combined, the weight of these crates sometimes exceeded 4,000 pounds. A special delivery truck equipped with a crane transported the glass from the warehouse to the delivery site. With his glass delivered, Pavel now had a shop ready for business.

In a short time he was busy cutting glass for new homes and decorative remodeling projects. His pleasant smile and friendly personality quickly won the confidence of customers. Many custom projects presented challenges he had never previously encountered, but with God's blessing each customer walked out of his door satisfied, many of them enthusiastically promoting the work of the youngest glazier in the country. His craftsmanship and attention to detail caused word to spread quickly that the new kid in town was "good." Soon his was one of the most successful glass businesses in town, with more customers than he could handle. After becoming established while juggling school and work, he earned more than double the salary of most men who worked all day and weekends.

Early each Friday afternoon he closed his shop until the following Monday. The promise of more money didn't entice him in the least to remain open for weekend business.

Pavel was considered one of the leaders at his church. His primary responsibility was the youth. Once a month he organized them as a worship team responsible for the entire service. He also enjoyed his position as director of the choir. Joining others in worship was his favorite part of the week; he wouldn't miss it for anything.

One day the large, imposing president of the co-op stepped into his shop to congratulate him on the success of his new business. With a smile he said, "Pavel, you are making a lot of money for us. We can't believe that you're able to do so well working only part-time. If school didn't stand in your way, you could no doubt double your profits. We want you to quit school and operate your business full-time."

"No, I can't do that," Pavel said, shaking his head.

"Why not? You have a great business with a good salary—what more could you want?" As he turned and walked toward the door he called over his shoulder, "If you think about it, I'm sure you will change your mind."

A couple of weeks later the president of the co-op returned, hoping his 17-year-old entrepreneur had considered the wisdom in his suggestion. To his dismay, he learned that Pavel hadn't entertained his proposition for even a moment. The president's friendly demeanor faded. In tones of obvious frustration he said, "You don't work in the mornings because you go to school. You don't work Saturdays because you go to church. You don't work Sundays because it's your free time. You simply have to start working weekends! That's the time most people make repairs on their homes."

"I already make a lot of money. I don't need to work weekends."

"You must have missed my point. I am not suggesting weekends as an option. I'm *telling* you it's mandatory."

"Well, I'm sorry, but I simply can't work weekends," Pavel said unflinchingly.

Once again the president exited the door, this time obviously displeased.

A week later he returned, determined to settle the weekend work issue. "I have a directive signed by my superiors insisting you begin to work on the weekends, effective immediately."

"I will begin working Sundays to satisfy the government, but I will not work Saturdays for anyone," Pavel replied firmly.

The next Sunday he began the new work schedule. After a couple of weeks the revenues proved the president's theory to be true. Now he was making even more money. Business was booming.

The co-op president returned once again. His presence in the doorway was beginning to be a regular occurrence. Without wasting time on small talk, he said, "I thought I made myself clear about you working Saturdays. I am getting tired of your disregarding my instructions. Now I hope I make myself clear. You *will* work Saturdays as well as Sundays. You have no choice."

"I can't."

"Nobody tells me no! What I say is the way it is! Refusing me is not an option!"

Calmly Pavel stood looking into the face of the official getting angrier by the minute.

"You listen to me! Either you work Saturdays or you are out of a job."

"That's up to you, I guess. I already told you I am not working, so it appears you are forcing me to quit."

Angrier than ever, the president stormed from the shop; there was nothing left to discuss. He hadn't supposed Pavel would be willing just to walk away from his profitable business. His bluff had backfired.

Glass Trouble

For a few weeks Pavel enjoyed the free time created by his closed business. However, after a month the president called on him again. This time he came with news that the name of his co-op was becoming tarnished because of deteriorating business. Not just the glass division was underperforming; each of the other areas had gone flat as well. The missing income from Pavel's glass shop only added to the dismal picture. Instead of being one of the top co-ops, they were now near the bottom. Pavel simply had to come back and reopen his shop. Agreeing, he opened his doors for business once again.

After a few weeks the president returned, his massive frame obscuring the doorway once again. He quickly made it apparent he was more determined than ever. This shop would be open for business on Saturdays!

"If you are not willing to choose to work Saturdays, I have decided to force you to," he began. His speech was beginning to sound like a record stuck in the same groove.

"I can't," stated Pavel.

"Don't you get stubborn and butt heads with me, because you'll lose."

"Listen, this is not about getting stubborn; I can't work Saturdays."

"Yes, you can."

"No, I can't."

"Yes, you can, and you *will*!" the president retorted. Nobody has ever treated me this way before! I will teach you a lesson you'll never forget! I am promising you that when I am finished with you, you will respect my authority and my commands. You wait and see—soon you will gladly follow my orders!" he shouted as he stomped through the door.

In a couple of weeks Pavel found his glass supply almost gone. It was the end of the week, and he would need more glass to resume business the following week. Calling the warehouse he placed his usual order for two crates of glass.

When he returned on Sunday, two familiar objects rested directly in front of his doorway. He never dreamed that in front of his shop he would see the two rotten crates that had been sitting outside the glass warehouse for the past two years. As men ordering glass had come and gone from the warehouse they had watched the wooden crates deteriorate month after month. As the months went by, the crates had become a joke as they sat rotting in the weather. Now here they were blocking his doorway.

A single rain could ruin an entire rack of glass. The changing temperature of moisture between the sheets would create such a powerful vacuum that the entire rack would become virtually welded together. These sheets had not encountered just one dose of rain but hundreds over the past two years. How anyone could have held the crumbling wood of the rotten crates together while transporting them from the warehouse was indeed a mystery.

Now he had two solid blocks of glass weighing 4,000 pounds each sitting in front of his door, with wooden shipping crates too rotten to move them. True to his word, the president of the co-op had arranged for this special shipment. He was planning to teach Pavel a lesson he would never forget.

Standing next to the crates of glass, he greeted Pavel with a sinister smile. "I had these crates of glass delivered here yesterday. When I dropped them off they were new, but look what has happened to them since you didn't come to work on Saturday. The responsibility is yours, since you weren't at work as you were instructed. In our country people are expected to work Saturdays," he said with a smirk. "You'd better fix this glass, or you'll have to pay for it. From here I am going to the courthouse to file a judgment against you. I'll give you 10 days to either fix the glass or pay for it in full. If you don't, you'll go to prison," he said with a sneer.

Pavel knew that the value of the glass was equivalent to three months' wages—far more than any government judgment against him. However, the prospect of prison was not an idle threat; people had gone to prison over missing money, even though they hadn't taken it.

If only he had saved some of the money he had earned. It had been "easy come, easy go." Rather than saving, he had gone on trips and frivolously purchased motorcycles, camping equipment, or whatever he desired at the moment. Now he was in a serious predicament. If only he had some of the money he had spent so freely, he wouldn't be in this situation.

Repeatedly he went to the president's office, attempting to reason with him. Each time the president only got angrier and more determined in his position. Pavel was either to repair the glass or to pay up. If he didn't, prison was waiting for him. And if Pavel came back for any more visits, the police would be on their way.

After a few days Pavel decided to brave one last visit to the president's office. Walking in, he began his final appeal. "You can put me in prison, but how will that benefit your co-op? You think you are going to make me work Saturdays and that by doing so your profits will double. But even if I lose my freedom I am not going to work Saturdays. So you can either withdraw your judgment or ruin my life. However, you know that your business will profit nothing with me in prison. Your profit margin will look even worse before the county audit committee. So what will you gain by going ahead with your plan? The bottom line is that I'm not going to work Saturdays. So why not let me increase my hours on Sunday and your numbers will increase accordingly? If you want me to, I will even increase my hours during the week," he pleaded.

"OK; if you return the two crates of glass undamaged and in good condition, I will let you continue your business. On the other hand, if the glass is damaged while you are handling it, you will have to pay for it in full. I am going to punish you and teach you a lesson I believe will change your mind. So go ahead and attempt to return the glass," he said with a baleful smile. Since the condition of the wooden crates made moving them impossible, his offer was nothing more than a foolproof trap.

For days Pavel had been praying, but now it felt as if his world would surely collapse on him. Seeing his long face, his father asked what was troubling him. After explaining his plight, he listened intently to his father share from his personal experience with God.

"You don't have to beg God. You told Him once about your need—don't you think He heard you?" he said. "You don't have to keep asking Him for the same thing over and over; just give your problem to Him."

"I don't know how to do that," Pavel said weakly.

"If you prayed once, don't ask Him for the same thing again and again. You told God you were giving Him permission to work. Why don't you let Him work in whatever way He sees best?"

"But nothing is happening."

"Well, God does not always answer on the schedule we have outlined for Him. You have to be patient as you wait for God. You don't want to be like King Saul. He waited seven days for Samuel the prophet's return to offer a sacrifice to God. He got tired of waiting for the prophet and decided to offer the sacrifice himself. You know the story—if only he would have waited just a little longer. When you pray, you need to trust God and not become impatient. He will answer in His time and in His way."

One last time Pavel went back to the co-op president's office to inform him of his final decision to not work Saturdays. "Whatever happens happens. Tomorrow I am having the glass crates shipped back to your warehouse."

That afternoon he hired a delivery truck with a crane to meet him at his shop. Not wanting to miss the disaster he was sure would take place, the president of the co-op, with some of his staff, came to witness the event. Waiting customers joined the ranks as spectators. Seeing a crowd gathering, several people happening by on the street decided to stop and watch as well.

When the delivery truck driver arrived and inspected the crates, he wanted no part in moving them. "These crates weigh about 4,000 pounds. These rotten crates will never hold together," he said, shaking his head.

"I will take full responsibility," Pavel assured him.

"I won't touch these crates unless you sign a release waiver for all liabilities."

With the document signed the leery driver swung his crane into position, dropping the cables down to the crates. Hooking them to the rigging blocks mounted on the first crate, he began the lift. Breathlessly Pavel watched as the slack left the cables and the rotten wooden crate lifted, gently swaying as it left the ground. Steadily the driver lifted the crate until it was about eight feet in the air.

Just as he was preparing to swing the crate to the truck, a startling crashing sound rang out. The bottom had suddenly dropped from the crate. The many long months of sitting in water and mud had taken its toll. With nothing to support it, the cube of welded glass sheets began a free fall. But to the amazement of all, it mysteriously halted its descent just beneath the crate. The bottomless crate swung back and forth above the 4,000-pound block of glass suspended in air!

In unison the crowd of spectators gasped. For a couple of long minutes no one dared to breathe. The entire crowd remained frozen in their tracks. Time stood still.

Pavel felt his knees begin to knock together beneath him. The driver, with his hands still on the controls of the crane, proved to be equally shaken. In tones barely above a whisper he asked, "What shall I do?"

"I don't know" was all Pavel could reply. All at once an idea came like a flash into his mind. "Lower the crate back over the glass," he instructed the driver. Slowly the driver lowered the crate back over the cube of suspended glass. As the crate completely enclosed the glass they descended in unison back to the ground.

The driver wrapped steel cables several times around the crate before lifting it to the bed of his truck. The spectators stood in silence as the truck drove away. They were unsure if they had been dreaming or if a giant mass of glass had just suspended itself in midair.

The president of the co-op came over to Pavel more stammering than talking. Pale and in shock, he attempted to form words. With his mouth quivering he whispered, "Just deliver the glass back to the warehouse. You don't need to worry about paying for it, and you don't need to worry about the report to the police. I will take care of everything. Just leave your business and never come back. And please don't curse me or my family." Turning, he walked away convinced that if the God Pavel served could suspend 4,000 pounds of glass in the air, He no doubt could deal unkindly with him and his family should Pavel so dictate.

From that miraculous day onward, Pavel repeatedly experienced God going before him, removing obstacles and solving problems as he put Him first. He never forgot God's beautiful promise: "If you put Me first, I will take care of you."

CHAPTER 4:

Where Are Your Books?

R*ing . . . Ring . . . Ring . . .*

"Who could be calling at 2:00 in the morning?" Mr. Goia wondered as he glanced at the alarm clock next to the bed. Fumbling for the phone in the darkness, his voice sounding half asleep, he managed to answer, "Hello, Goias."

"*You have no time to spare! Get your books out of your house!*" the voice on the other end blurted.

"Who is this?" Mr. Goia asked, now wide awake.

"I can't tell you. What I'm telling you is that there's no time for you to talk! It's *urgent*—get your books out *now*!

The buzz of the dial tone coming from the receiver signaled that the call had ended.

"Everybody get up! Hurry! There's no time to waste!" Mr. Goia called loudly to his sleeping family. "The secret service police are on their way over to search our house for religious books!"

Pavel and his sisters jumped from their beds, joining their parents already responding to the emergency. No one needed to tell them that this was serious. The Goia family had one of the most exhaustive spiritual libraries in the country. Numerous translations of the Bible, sets of commentaries, and inspired books lined the walls of Mr. Goia's study. These books were the primary resource for the church when copying was possible. Frantically the books were pulled from shelves and shoved in boxes.

When the first few boxes were full, Mr. Goia ran them out to the sidecar of his motorcycle. Calling over his shoulder as loudly as he dared, he instructed them to keep boxing and that he would be back in a few minutes. Without even taking time to zip his jacket, he sped away with his precious cargo.

In record time the motorcycle returned from Grandpa Goia's farm just outside of town for another load. Trip after trip the motorcycle sped away, loaded with books. Relieved, the exhausted packing team quickly loaded the last box of books into the sidecar to be taken to the safe haven in the country.

Not until the motorcycle had been returned to its parking spot did Mr. Goia dare to relax enough to exhale. He was equally exhausted, but the family had won the race against time. Kneeling together they thanked God for protecting His books and them. Standing to their feet, they turned out the lights, anxious to accept the invitation of their waiting sheets.

Bang! Bang! Bang!! The front door shook as pounding fists announced the intended entrance of a visitor. The Goia family hadn't even had time to pull the covers over them when the rattling front door informed them that those waiting on the other side had not come for a social call.

"We have a warrant to search your house for religious books," declared a plain clothes officer. Mr. Goia looked past the officer to the waiting search party. From the look on their faces it was plain to see they had come for business.

"We have information leading us to believe that you are keeping a large supply of illegal religious books," the officer said as he stepped into the house, pushing Mr. Goia aside. In an instant the small army of plain clothes officers wearing black gloves filed into the house, already beginning to move furniture, pictures, and rugs. Diligently they searched every place suspect for hiding books.

After a few minutes of unsuccessful searching, Mr. Goia began challenging them as Elijah had the prophets of Baal on Mount Carmel: "Surely you are trained in your work; if you have come for books, why aren't you finding them?"

"We'll find your books! Just stay out of our way," the frustrated chief inspector snapped.

They intensified their search. To the chief's dismay, Mr. Goia continued to question their competency while they dismantled his house. After turning it upside down, the frustrated officers came up empty-handed. When the chief inspector finally called an end to the search, they appeared grateful to leave, as it also signaled an end to the humiliation provided by Mr. Goia. The critiquing of their proficiency had been less than pleasant, though Mr. Goia appeared to have enjoyed it.

As the lights of the police cars disappeared, the Goia family returned to their knees in thankfulness for the providence of God in their behalf.

This time they really did fall fast asleep. Tomorrow would mean cleaning up an unbelievable mess, but it was OK, because God's books were safe.

Although Pavel was still in high school, he had already experienced more testing of his faith than most would in a lifetime. The resistance from the government was relentless, providing his family with obstacle after obstacle. But together with the other believers the Goias covenanted to remain faithful in their worship and in sharing their faith.

Bibles were nearly impossible to obtain. Some of the newer believers had never even held a Bible in their hands. Meeting together in prayer, the leaders decided upon an extremely dangerous solution.

A contact was made outside the country as a source for Bibles. When visas were obtained, a quick "business trip" was scheduled. Returning to the church, the door panels of the car were removed, revealing the hidden treasure.

The next week at church no one said a word about new Bibles. Many elated worshippers, however, found one waiting for them in the pew where they regularly sat. Several successful endeavors encouraged them to proceed with a much riskier plan.

One of the church members had a business requiring him to make frequent business trips across the border with his van. It was a perfect opportunity to expand their underground smuggling operation. For several nights, in the cover of darkness, his van was converted to a Bible-smuggling van. A professional welder created a false bottom for the van that perfectly resembled the original. Now they had the capacity to transport Bibles, not a dozen at a time, but by the boxload.

The Bible smuggling operation was in process when Pavel received a call from the local chief of secret service police. He wanted to hire him to tune the piano in his home. As a little side business Pavel had begun piano tuning. His keen ear for tone and his love for music had made him one of the best piano tuners in the area.

By the time the piano was tuned, a small bond of friendship had developed between him and the officer. "I like you, Pavel. You are a good kid," the officer said with a smile. "Is there anything I can do for you?" Having grown up with a government system riddled with corruption, bribes, and favors, Pavel understood perfectly what he was implying.

"No, I don't need anything."

"Well, let me just give you a little inside information anyway. Your congregation has 27 informers working for us. I just thought you might find that information useful," he said as Pavel prepared to leave.

"Thank you for your business and the tip," Pavel said, stepping out the door.

Pavel's inside information reminded the church leaders that their Bible-smuggling operation would be exposed if the wrong members overheard something. With extreme caution the plans for the first "business trip" using the newly designed van proceeded.

The small group of men waiting in the darkness behind the church wondered, Had he made it through? Carefully they studied the lights coming from the approaching vehicle. Seeing the headlights turn off and the van continue to the back of the church enabled them to exhale in relief.

Box after box was removed from the secret compartment. None of them had ever seen this many Bibles at one time in all their lives. They were overjoyed as they unloaded the last box, realizing how many families would be blessed with the first Bible of their very own.

The next question was where to hide them. Churches were often searched, so the hiding place would have to be a good one. Some of the places they had previously used for a few Bibles were now out of the question because of the greatly increased quantity. They simply couldn't think of a place large enough for a shipment this size. "What about the steeple?" someone suggested. After further thought they decided the steeple would probably be first on the list if the church were searched.

"How about the woodshed?" suggested another. Walking out to the woodshed, which was half full of firewood, they agreed it was their best option. Quickly removing the piles of wood, they stacked the boxes of Bibles in its place. With the wood restacked in the shed they returned to their homes and prayed for God's special protection for the hidden treasure.

The following weekend the youth had a church picnic. They played games and enjoyed a nice meal provided at lunch time. For a special treat a number of watermelons were sliced and served. With juice running down their faces and arms they ate their watermelon while running from place to place around the church. They really enjoyed the treat.

When the social was over and the youth had gone home, the leaders stayed behind for the last of the cleanup. Pavel cringed as he looked in the direction of the woodshed with the door partly ajar. Opening the door for inspection, he was dismayed to discover that several had chosen the woodshed as a depository for their melon rinds. "What a mess," he exclaimed, calculating the cleanup time. As youth leaders they would have to come back later to clean it up. It was late, and everyone was ready to go home.

One MIRACLE After Another

A few days later an ominous message quickly circulated among the church leaders. "The police are at the church! They have been tipped that a large shipment of Bibles are hidden at the church!" The men prayed as they hurried to see what would happen to their treasure. Watching safely from a distance, they prayed earnestly that God would protect His Written Word.

How thankful they were that the steeple had not been chosen as the hiding place; police officers could be seen overturning everything in their search high above the church. For some time the search continued inside the church. After feeling confident that nothing had been hidden inside, the officers began looking for anything suspicious around the churchyard.

The hidden spectators watched breathlessly as one of the police officers walked to the woodshed. Opening the door, he jumped back. A swarm of angry yellow jackets buzzed around his head, not pleased that their melon feast had been interrupted. The melon rinds appeared to have invited every yellow jacket within five miles to a party. Consequently the woodshed had become more like a beehive than an edifice containing dismembered trees waiting to warm church members during the cold winter months.

"There's nothing out here but a big wasps' nest," the officer called to the others as he made his escape from a swarm of diving yellow jackets. Ducking and swatting he ran back to join the other officers.

Feeling defeated, but confident that Bibles were nowhere on the church property, the police officers got into their cars and left.

The church leaders breathed a sigh of relief. Their faith grew stronger as they realized God could use even youthful carelessness to guard His precious Word.

As the need arose, additional "business trips" were planned. Each mission was an extremely dangerous undertaking, but this praying group of church leaders knew they were working with God. And how rewarding it was to see the smiling face on one of His children clutching her newfound treasure!

CHAPTER 5:

You Don't Exist

W*hat am I going to do with my life?* Pavel wondered. *I've dreamed of becoming a pastor most of my life. But that seems rather unrealistic since seminaries have been all but eliminated by Communism. Besides, why should I have a miserable life when I don't need to?* he reasoned.

Perhaps I should become a music teacher . . . or an engineer, he thought as he pondered the path that would define his life. Carefully he evaluated each option. *I have always loved music. Maybe I should make that my life study. On the other hand, if I became an engineer I could not only get a good job but design my own house. The years I have spent working with my father in the building business would surely prove advantageous to me as an engineer.* For several days he wrestled with what career he should pursue.

Pavel was not excited about another obstacle to his dreams. High school would soon be over, and a trip to the military draft registration center was mandatory for every young man 18 years of age. A stiff prison sentence awaited those not taking the time to register or thinking to opt out of the military. Before continuing his education, he would have to serve his country.

The government had two options for military service. Just nine months of service was required for those able to pass the entrance exam at one of the universities, which was much more attractive than the second option. For those not attending university, a year and a half of military service was required. He would need to decide on a career soon. The shorter option was an easy first choice for all, but it was even more than just a good idea for a Christian.

The military made no exceptions for those desiring to serve God. Pavel had heard enough stories to know that remaining faithful to God would be the most difficult experience he would ever face. In spite of what undoubtedly awaited him he would have to make a trip to the military registration center as soon as possible. Without a registration card, his life would be on hold. This card was required for everything from getting a driver's license to applying at the university. He could not put it off another day; he needed his card.

"I would like to fill out my draft registration card," Pavel said as he approached the officer attending the front desk.

"Fill out this form using your full name," instructed the officer. After completing the form, he placed it on the counter to be processed.

"Pavel Goia," repeated the officer quietly to himself as he walked over to the filing cabinets lining the wall.

After several minutes of searching file cabinet drawers, the officer looked up in obvious frustration. "This is impossible," he said, looking up from the last cabinet. "Nothing like this has ever happened as long as I have worked here. Our records are updated and audited on a regular basis, but we have no file for you. You simply don't exist; it is as if you were never born," he said in disbelief.

The whole thing seemed a bit humorous to Pavel. He smiled, thinking about all that could be enjoyed by a person never having to face consequences. If he didn't really exist, what could be done to him?

"So, then, what you are saying is that if I hit you right now, there is nothing you can do to me, because I'm not really here," Pavel joked.

"I don't think that would be one of your brighter moments. If you try it, you'll find out in a hurry that I am very much here. You exist, all right—I just can't find you in our system. I'm sorry. There's nothing I can do for you," the puzzled officer concluded.

Pavel stood there wondering what to do next. He had always *thought* he existed. It was an entirely new concept to discover that his existence had really just been an illusion.

"Well, if I don't exist, at least I won't have to go to the military. That's good news," he said, seeing the bright side of the moment. All at once he remembered his reason for coming. He needed his registration card in order to apply at the university. "The bad news is that I wouldn't be able to go to school," he stated seriously.

"That's right," agreed the officer. "They would put you in prison for missing your time in the military. You must come back on your own to register."

"Aren't you getting confused as to who would go to prison?" Pavel countered. "I just came to register and you didn't do it, so it would be *you* going to prison. You need to find me. I can't go to school without my registration card. I just can't leave here without it. You *have* to do something," Pavel pleaded.

The officer disappeared into the next room for a moment, returning with the general. After a quick briefing, the general took his turn searching each file cabinet, but the documents were nowhere to be found.

The general went over to the desk for a pen and paper. "I am going to write you a note of temporary exemption so that you can register for the university. But you must promise me that you'll come back again after we have had time to look for your documents. I'm not supposed to do this, but I'm going to trust you to come back," he said with a smile. Pavel thanked him and assured him he would come back. Armed with a note bearing the general's signature, he walked out the door thanking and praising God.

With several years of construction experience already in place, surely becoming a building engineer would be his best choice. His next step would be to make application to the university for his engineering degree. He was going to become a building engineer!

In Communist Romania, however, this would not be an easy task. Only a handful of the brightest students would be accepted for each degree offered. He was all too familiar with the system. His sister had been studying music and practicing the piano for many years for one of the positions offered in music. The only possibility of reaching the required excellence was to hire a private tutor. Each lesson was followed by daily practice sessions lasting eight hours. This had been her diligent pursuit—not for months, but for many long years. At last, with God's blessing she had achieved her goal. From the 1,200 applicants auditioning for the opportunity to study piano at the university, she had been awarded one of the five positions. Pavel was proud of his sister's prestigious accomplishment. What brother wouldn't be?

He knew it would be equally challenging to be accepted to one of the universities offering a degree in engineering. Only the top 10 applicants would be accepted. With such overwhelming odds, only straight-A students dared to enroll for the qualifying exam. Even though Pavel had been at the top of his class since entering grade school, he knew this would be competition as he had never seen before. How thankful he was for his friendship with the all-knowing God of the universe. In earnest prayer he submitted his plan to Him.

As he prayed and studied for the next few mornings, the story of Daniel and his three friends came vividly before him. God had blessed them with a wisdom far surpassing every other student in the land because of their faithfulness. In every category their wisdom was discovered to be 10 times that of the other youth. Pavel repeatedly invited God to bless him in the same way if it would bring honor and glory to His name.

With his note bearing the general's signature he set out to enroll in a nearby university. After listening to his brief explanation, the registrar refused his request. No exceptions would be granted at her school. Either you had your registration card or you didn't apply. Pavel couldn't help feeling a little disappointed, but since there were other universities, he would just try another one. But one by one, each registrar offered a similar response: no registration card, no application.

After attempting to register at 15 universities without success, his prospects appeared bleak. There was only one more university offering a degree relating to construction. *But why even bother?* he thought gloomily. Discouragement deepened with each city block he walked. His feet scuffed along the pavement, shuffling forward without purpose. *Why has God let me down?* he wondered. He had faithfully opened door after door for him—until now. In darkness and gloom it felt as if he had been forgotten.

Deciding he had nothing to lose, he aimed his shuffling feet in the direction of the last university. Late in the afternoon he approached the registrar's desk. "I have come to apply for the building engineering course," he began. Without waiting for the rejection he was sure would follow, he proceeded to tell the woman that he was sure she wouldn't want him either, that he might as well save her the trouble of rejecting him too.

When he finally ended his miserable speech, the woman smiled kindly at him and said, "I will let you apply. It's not your fault your papers have been lost." In his gloom he didn't even hear her kind words. *Why wait around for words of doom*? he grumbled, turning and heading for the door.

"Wait!" called the registrar. "I said I will let you apply."

Pavel stopped. "You will? Are you sure you won't get into trouble?" he stammered.

"You let me take care of my business. Do you want to apply or not?" she asked with a sparkle in her eye. Within a few moments Pavel was on his way home. He was registered for school. How thankful he was that he had not given up in discouragement. Maybe God had not forgotten him after all.

He had just three months to study for the entrance exams. And study he did. From morning until night, day after day he pored over every resource material he could find. At the end of three months he had completed eight mathematics books and four physics books, each designed as full-year courses. He had prayed for wisdom and done all in his power to fill his mind with knowledge. Now the rest was up to God.

As the date for the engineering exam drew near, each applicant received an overview for final preparation. The exam would be administered over two days, one day for mathematics and the other for physics. The mathematics exam would include algebra, calculus, trigonometry, and geometry. The physics exam would cover hydraulics, mechanics, electricity, and molecular physics. Pavel knew he would need God's help to be one of the university's top 10 applicants.

Before leaving for his first exam, he kept his daily morning appointment with God. He knew better than to leave home alone. With peace and the assurance that God was with him he entered the classroom.

The math test was first. He was amazed how clearly he understood each problem and its answer. With confidence he quickly solved each one. In just half the allotted time he walked forward with his completed exam. He could tell that God had blessed his mind with the wisdom he had requested.

Feeling certain he could also complete the second exam early, he purchased his return train ticket home for 2:40 p.m., even though the test was scheduled to end at 4:00 p.m. He knew he might be cutting it a bit close as it was a one- to one-and-a-half hour bus ride from the university to the train station, depending on the traffic. If he finished in half the time again, he would make it without any problem. With a nonrefundable ticket he would need to make sure to finish early.

Beginning his physics exam, he realized that the ease with which he had taken the previous test had vanished. He was really struggling. His mind felt blank. Today, in place of instant understanding, he had none.

This can't be happening! he thought in a state of panic. The professor had given his students the option of taking test A or B. He had selected test A. After 15 minutes of staring blankly at test A, he asked if he could exchange his test for the other. The professor made the exchange but warned him that no other changes would be made.

Diligently he pored over his new exam. Slowly the answers began to come to his mind. Finally, at 2:30 in the afternoon, he finished his last problem. He was in a real bind now. His train was scheduled to leave in just a few minutes. He had no time for the one-hour bus ride to the train station; he would have to catch a taxi. Anxiously he prayed, "Lord, please help me make it to the station in time."

He waved frantically for a cab. Jumping in, he breathlessly pleaded for the driver to go as fast as he could to the North Train Station.

"Did you say to drive as fast as I can?" asked the driver. "I don't think you know how fast that is." A broad smile broke out across the driver's face as he repeated the request: "As fast as I can. Get in sonny; you'll never forget this ride as long as you live," the cab driver promised with a smirk.

Before Pavel had time to shut his door the tires squealed on the pavement beneath them. Racing toward the traffic ahead, he was sure the driver would have to slow down before reaching the maze of cars, trucks, and buses that filled the street. Slow down? Not this driver. He needed only one pedal—the accelerator.

Flying along this busy boulevard at four times the speed of the other traffic was more than Pavel had bargained for. He had heard of cars traveling like this on four lane highways, but at least everyone was traveling the same speed. He held on for dear life. With white knuckles he clutched anything he could grip, trying desperately to keep from flying around inside the car—or worse yet, out the window. In and out of cars and trucks they wildly weaved.

"Surely a stripe of paint from each vehicle they passed had been embedded along the sides of the taxi," Pavel concluded as he held on for dear life. The possibility of their "yellow cab" being transformed to a "rainbow cab" did not seem all that remote.

"Now what?" Pavel wondered as he glanced through the windshield at the busy intersection directly in front of them. He didn't have long to wait, as his driver, consumed by his mission, swerved abruptly to miss the car in front of them, whose driver had somehow come to the conclusion that a red traffic light meant to stop.

With his head jerking back and forth the cabbie searched madly for which bus or truck to squeeze between, all the while keeping his hand on the horn. Swerving wildly to avoid oncoming cars from either side, the driver continued his mad dash. Several drivers responded with their horns just in case the crazy cabbie had not seen their expressions of displeasure or heard their shouts.

Exploding through intersections without slowing down and ignoring red lights left Pavel cringing. With the rest of the traffic stopped at the red light that his driver had interpreted as *go*, the boulevard opened ahead of them for some distance. This provided a real run at the unsuspecting victims ahead.

Suddenly the driver tipped his head back, and with a burst of laughter repeated, "As fast as I can?" Looking over at Pavel, he asked for clarification. "Do you want me to go faster?" Weakly Pavel shook his head side to side, whispering "No—*please* don't go any faster." Again the driver laughed as he looked over at his passenger, who now looked more like a ghost than a mortal.

Something ahead had caused a traffic jam. Cars were backed up for almost the whole city block. Seeing the impossibility of getting through the mass of vehicles, the driver spotted an alternate route. Without warning he swerved to the right, hitting his brakes for the first time since the ride began. With all four tires loudly squealing and barely missing the end of the waiting cars, they skidded to the side of the road. When the cab hit the curb, Pavel's helpless body flew to the roof, then back to his seat. His white knuckles had not managed to hold him in place during this maneuver.

With his head tipped back once again, his driver repeated, "As fast as I can?" Down the sidewalk they raced past the waiting cars, sending screaming pedestrians and sidewalk vendors in all directions. Pavel felt like joining them, but he was unable to speak, let alone get out a real scream.

Arriving at the intersection by sidewalk, they shot out between heavy cross-traffic once again with horn blowing and swerving violently back and forth, nearly being sandwiched between vehicles coming from both directions. On the other side of the intersection, the taxicab-turned-racecar was back on course, speeding through the city. Pavel wondered if he would live to see the train station, let alone actually ride home on one of the cars.

At last the station came into view. *There is no way even this taxi driver can get us through this one,* Pavel thought with sinking heart. Another massive traffic jam had cars backed up for what might as well have been a mile. This time it appeared there would be no escape route. Perhaps his death-defying journey had been in vain.

But once again Pavel had underestimated the creativity of his driver. The boulevard on which they were racing was divided in the center by two sets of train tracks, one for incoming passengers and the other for outgoing. The southbound train was due to depart immediately, but the northbound track was empty. With trains constantly coming and going, even the empty tracks appeared to be out of the question.

But rising to the occasion, the taxi driver quickly headed for the vacant track. Timing was now everything. Racing down the tracks alongside the waiting cars was bad enough, but the inbound and outbound trains would be passing at any moment. Even bouncing up and down the train tracks could not diminish the realization that they could be sandwiched between two trains any second. With only a split second to spare the taxi jumped over the tracks, cutting in front of the long line of cars waiting to enter the station.

In a cloud of dust the driver slid into the station at the very lane of Pavel's waiting train. To his amazement, it had been delayed. As he climbed out of the car the delayed train began to depart. In a flash he grabbed his bag and made a mad dash to catch the train gaining speed ahead of him. Over his shoulder he thought he heard his driver laughingly call out to him, "Was that fast enough?"

By the time Pavel reached the moving train, its momentum and his own were the same. With one mighty leap he jumped aboard. Collapsing into an empty seat, he thanked his heavenly Father. "Dear God, thank You for sparing my life in that amazing taxi ride and for delaying the train just long enough for me to make it." Never had he been so grateful to catch a train before! He was alive and on his way home.

The date for the exam results finally came. Eagerly Pavel scanned the roster for his name. How had he fared against such heavy competition? He found his name near the top of the list. He had scored fourth of the 87 applicants taking the exam. The asterisk beside his name indicated he had been accepted as a building engineer student. What an honor! he smiled to himself. Pavel knew it was God who had blessed him, just as He had blessed the faithful Hebrew youth in Bible times.

Recognizing Pavel, the registrar smiled as he approached her desk. "You are one lucky young man," she said.

"I know—I passed!" he responded with a grin from ear to ear.

"No, that's not what I mean. The military is beginning a pilot program today that will include only those students accepted to this university. Each of our students will be enrolled in the special school that until now has been only for family members of high-ranking officers. The army is a very difficult experience at best, but those who attend this program will enjoy many privileges that the rest do not. So, you see, if the military hadn't lost your file, you would've been accepted at one of the other universities, and you wouldn't have been able to be a part of this elite new program. Your timing was absolutely perfect!" she ended, beaming with delight. The chance she had taken on this young man had given him the opportunity of a lifetime.

Leaving the registration office, Pavel began to pray. "Lord, how could I have ever doubted You? When everything started going wrong, I thought You had forgotten me. Please help me to trust You even in the dark and lonely times when You are silent. When everything goes wrong at once, it feels like it would be impossible for anything good to work out. I just want to thank You for keeping Your promise to me. You worked for my good when I really didn't deserve it. You are such an amazing Father. If the woman at the university only knew You, she would know that there is no such thing as luck. You really do have a plan for my life." With a smile he made his way home. His God had proved faithful once again.

The officer at the military registration center smiled as he saw Pavel walking back into his office. "We found your file a few days ago," he announced with a bit of relief in his voice. "Just before you came to register we had begun painting our office. All the filing cabinets had to be moved around in order for the painter to access the walls. While one of the cabinets was being moved a drawer fell out, spilling files all over the floor. We thought we had returned all the files to the drawer, but obviously we had missed yours. A few days ago we finished the remodeling project. As we moved the cabinets back to the wall we spotted a file. It was yours. It evidently slid underneath one of the cabinets during the spill. Now you exist. You really were born after all," the officer explained with a twinkle in his eye.

At the end of the officer's explanation, the general looked up from his paperwork with some encouragement of his own. "Pavel, you did an excellent job on your exams. You scored very well among our nation's best students. Without the exemption note, you would never have been able to apply at the university. As a result of your excellent test scores you'll have to spend only nine months in the military, and at our best institution. I'm glad I trusted you."

"So am I," Pavel agreed with a smile as he walked toward the door.

Though he was thankful for a shorter term, the fact remained that he still had to serve in the military. It wasn't long until he found himself boarding the train bound for the army base in Rânicu Vâlcea.

As the train slowly wound its way back and forth up the steep pass over the Retezat Mountains he tried to imagine what it was going to be like in the military while remaining true to the Captain of the Lord of hosts. Quietly he prayed to the Commander of the universe, "Lord, as captain of the hosts of heaven help me to be true to You as my highest commanding officer. Help me to remember who is really in charge. I want to be a faithful soldier in Your army here on earth."

CHAPTER 6:

No Longer Free

As Pavel stepped off the train to the waiting military transport trucks, he knew this was it—he was now in the army.

"Did I tell you to sit down? *Stand up*!" ordered the army colonel.

Startled and unsure of what move to make next, Pavel quickly jumped to his feet. Wide-eyed he stared across the large wooden desk into the stone face of the high-ranking military officer. The secret service police officers flanking his sides created a very intimidating atmosphere. The whole situation felt very unnerving for an 18-year-old soldier.

The drab and barren office labeled "Security" on the door needed nothing more than the stories preceding it to intimidate any who should be unfortunate enough to enter. For those growing up in a Communist country it was a fearful experience to encounter the secret service police for any reason. If this office were intended to be the welcoming portion of military orientation, it certainly was a miserable failure.

Looking sternly across the table at Pavel, the colonel continued: "We know you. We know what you eat. We know what you say. And we know how you dress. We know where you live and everything about your family. If you would like, we can tell you what you said yesterday on the telephone. I hope you are getting the message. We know everything about you. We know that you are an Adventist. But it really doesn't matter what you believe. You are no longer free! From now on we will tell you what to do and when to do it. You are under our command.

"Goia, I hope I have made myself clear. You will do as you are told. As soon as you refuse to work on Saturday or start preaching your ridiculous beliefs to those around you, you will be sent to prison!

"You will obey every order from your commanding officer. If you refuse, be assured that you'll go directly to prison. In our prisons we know how to teach young men like you how to obey. You'll be beaten *repeatedly* until you learn that it is useless to resist." A sinister smile replaced the officer's stern look as he prepared to finish his presentation.

Pavel listened breathlessly to the ominous prospects facing anyone who stood for his faith in the military. There was no doubt in his mind that the officer meant every word he was saying. Memories of a close family friend who had experienced the speech still ringing in his ears came vividly before him. Remaining faithful to God had cost many before him their lives.

"Goia, there simply is no way around it; there is no way to escape our authority. You had better decide here and now to give up all that foolishness about God. You're in the army now. You no longer have the freedom to think or choose for yourself. We'll do that for you," concluded the officer in a snide tone of voice.

Pavel closed the door behind him with the realization that he was about to experience a real testing of his faith. Thoughtfully he made his way across the courtyard to the barracks.

The initiation process had not been all that pleasant thus far. The next portion wasn't much better. Standing unclothed before medical personnel for a detailed inspection of his anatomy, he felt invaded and humiliated. They inspected his body with such amazing scrutiny that they no doubt knew more about it than he did. Not a flea or tick could have hidden from their inspecting eye.

Next came the power wash. They called it a "shower." Surely an automobile in a car wash would lose its paint if subjected to the rigorous scrubbing he endured. His skin felt as if it would be peeled right off his body. No doubt about it—he was *clean.*

Rubbing his hand over his head, he felt the place where hair used to reside. His now-bald head was the finished product of what had been termed a "haircut" by the military barber.

Dressed in dark-green military fatigues, he couldn't help feeling as if every part of his identity had just been stripped away. Initiation completed, he could only wonder what would come next.

Lying on his cot that night, Pavel thought about what a difference this one day had made in his life. He was just a six-hour train ride over the mountains from home, but at that moment it felt as if he were on the other side of the world. What was his family doing while he looked up in the darkness from his cot? Many warm memories of home, family, and friends flooded his mind. Thoughts of home caused loneliness to knock at his heart's door. Bravely he fought it away. He was a soldier now.

The smell of the fresh cookies and treats beneath him in his duffel bag only added to the memories of his loving family. Each of them in their own special way had encouraged him to be faithful. He smiled as he felt assured that they had prayed for him throughout the day.

A warm feeling came over him as he realized that this was the time his family would be gathering together for family worship. How blessed he had been to grow up in a family so rich in faith and Christian heritage.

But one memory above all others made him long for home—Dana. Since he was 6 years old he had loved the sparkle in her eyes. He had informed her with all the dignity a 6-year-old could muster that he was going to marry her. She had not immediately shared his commitment. Since she was only 3 at the time, she no doubt would need a few years to obtain his maturity. He would just have to wait. And wait he did.

How thankful he was now that she had come to share his dream. He retraced every detail of her face in his mind. The little sparkle in her eye at 3 had changed to something much more captivating in recent years. As only a young man in love can do, Pavel tried to picture every one of her fine features. Most important her love for God was deep and true. As she bade him farewell she had promised him he would always be in her thoughts and prayers.

Feeling the love of his family and friends, Pavel closed his eyes to rest. The power of their prayers had followed him.

Early the next morning he awoke to pray for God's presence and companionship throughout the day. Since having any religious material was strictly forbidden he was without his Bible. Thankful that he had begun very early to memorize many portions of Scripture, passage after passage came back to his mind. Even though he couldn't actually hold his Bible, in his mind he could see the pages marked and underlined. As God spoke His Word back to Pavel, he felt the courage he needed to begin a new day in his new world so far away from the one he had left behind.

After breakfast the new recruits were gathered for orientation. They received briefings about each of the areas of training their garrison provided. Each day there were overviews of the programs in which they would be involved. Much detail was given concerning policies and procedures. The army spent ample time detailing discipline and penalties for noncompliance. For disobeying an order in the presence of a commanding officer there were stiff penalties. However, if a soldier should disobey an officer in the presence of one or more other soldiers, the penalty doubled.

All week the sessions continued. At the end of the week one point had been clearly reinforced: each soldier would do exactly as he was told.

The very first day to begin work following the week of orientation was Saturday. After breakfast the vast courtyard filled with lines of soldiers facing their commanding officers.

As the line began to form for Pavel's unit he took his place next to a friend he recognized from church. Both of them had been dreading this moment all week. Side by side they stood facing their lieutenant. Since arriving at the garrison they had wondered what would happen when this moment finally came.

Facing the 51 men before him, the lieutenant dictated the work orders for the day. A large delivery of fuel in 55-gallon barrels needed to be taken to the gas station and stacked in orderly rows.

After completing a few minor instructions, the lieutenant walked directly over to Pavel and his friend. "I'm going to keep my eye on both of you today, and you will work. Just as soon as you refuse my order, I will see to it that you go straight to prison."

Pavel prayed earnestly, "Lord, tell me what I should do. I need Your help." Shaken by the threat of prison, the friend next to him whispered, "Let's just go ahead and work for a while, and later we can stop."

"No. I'm not going to go against my conscience," Pavel whispered back.

At that moment a strong impression came to his mind: "Go to the restroom." After stating his need to use the restroom, the lieutenant agreed, with the stipulation that he return immediately. Without a reply Pavel made his way to his Sabbath retreat.

Locking himself into one of the stalls, he began to pray. As he prayed, the story from Daniel 3 began to replay in his mind. The faithfulness of Shadrach, Meshach, and Abednego while facing the death sentence inspired him with new courage. Their answer before a heathen king came back to him in all its boldness.

"Now if ye be ready that at what time ye hear the sound of the cornet, flute, harp, sackbut, psaltery, and dulcimer, and all kinds of musick, ye fall down and worship the image which I have made; well: but if ye worship not, ye shall be cast the same hour into the midst of a burning fiery furnace; and who is that God that shall deliver you out of my hands? Shadrach, Meshach, and Abednego, answered and said to the king, O Nebuchadnezzar, we are not careful to answer thee in this matter. If it be so, our God whom we serve is able to deliver us from the burning fiery furnace, and he will deliver us out of thine hand, O king. But if not, be it known unto thee, O king, that we will not serve thy gods, nor worship the golden image which thou hast set up" (verses 15-18).

Never had this story meant so much as it did as he sat locked in a bathroom stall in order to remain faithful to God's day of rest.

Pavel did not have to think back to Bible times. His father and grandfather had repeated to him many of their own experiences. One story in particular encouraged him as he prayed. He could almost hear his grandfather's voice as the details of his story began to replay in his mind.

It was no secret that Christianity was considered an enemy to Communist Romania. The teaching that God created and loved humanity directly undermined the philosophy and security of the Communist government. As a result, diligent efforts were put in place to cripple and extinguish, if possible, every Christian organization.

There were only a handful of Christians remaining after the persecution in Grandpa Goia's day. Each time a meeting was planned it was with utmost secrecy. No one knew whom to trust. In some cities three out of every 10 persons worked as informers for the secret service police. The neighbor you thought you could trust might be relaying everything he saw and heard. A gathering with more than 10 persons was considered suspect even in a shopping center or marketplace, and the participants would be arrested and interrogated to determine their agenda.

Everyone lived in a state of constant fear. Merciless beatings and tortures were often performed in full view of the public as a reminder of the punishment for crimes against the government—Christianity being one of the worst! Death was not uncommon for those beaten by the secret service police. Those who survived endured disabilities for the rest of their lives. These living realities were constant reminders. Sharing Christianity was as dangerous as spying.

In a neighboring village the only remaining church member had just died. Grandpa Goia was considered the church leader in the absence of a pastor. The members earnestly desired a Christian burial for their resting friend. But the consequences for holding such a meeting were understood by all. Death by beating would undoubtedly follow.

Gathering the few remaining church members together, Grandpa Goia made plans for a funeral, in spite of the imminent retribution. He reassured the fearful members that he would take full responsibility whatever the cost. He knew the price all too well, as he himself had been interrogated and disciplined by the secret service police for encouraging Christianity.

Word had spread throughout the village that a Christian funeral would take place the following day for their resting neighbor and friend. The next morning in the front yard of their beloved friend Grandpa Goia stood with his Bible next to the casket. People began coming from everywhere. It wasn't long until everyone in the village crowded around the yard. Most had never attended a Christian funeral. Some came out of respect, but most were just curious.

Sensing a special opportunity and an empowering from above, Grandpa Goia began to share the plan of salvation and the blessed hope waiting for those who accepted the offered gift of eternal life. For most this was the first time they had ever heard about a Creator God who loved each of them personally. He told of a love so great that the God in heaven left His throne above to come and die on a cruel cross to pay the debt for each of their sins. All who chose to accept the gift of eternal life would soon be raised to life, never to die again. Earnestly he appealed to the villagers as his own congregation. If any should have a desire to learn more they could feel free to contact him.

Learning of the illegal assembly, the police responded by enlisting a group of the village drunks as enforcers. When the funeral was nearing completion, the police, with their special task force, arrived. Repeatedly they attempted to press through the crowd to reach Grandpa Goia and those leading out in the funeral, but the villagers were pressed so tightly together that it was impossible for them to make their way through.

Reluctantly they waited for the service to end. As they waited they waved their large, menacing clubs. They paced back and forth as they waited for the opportunity to remind all in attendance what could be expected for such blatant disregard of government policy. There would be no mercy. Sooner or later those conducting the service would have to leave.

When Grandpa Goia finished his appeal, the crowd parted, forming a long corridor for the exit of those carrying the casket. The police officers, flanked by their drunken task force, moved quickly into the vacated spaces. Both sides of the passageway were lined with men eager to use their raised clubs.

Villagers and church members alike waited breathlessly for the inevitable beating death of those responsible for the funeral. For a few moments time stood still.

Praying silently, Grandpa Goia courageously stepped forward and began walking toward the corridor with the waiting death squad. Just as he had promised, he declared himself to be the one responsible for the meeting. Eyes filled with hatred glared back at him. Step by step he moved closer to the cursing threats.

His next step would possibly be the last he would ever take. Continuing to pray silently he stepped forward. To his amazement, the cursing threats stopped, and the raised clubs were lowered. The angry faces of just a moment ago had in an instant become pale. The eyes of his proud assailants were now wide with a fear of their own. Each of the armed men quickly backed a few steps away when Grandpa Goia came near.

The village chief of police waited at the end of the line with his own wide eyes as Grandpa Goia passed by, signaling those carrying the casket to follow. In wonder the villagers watched as the church members finished at the graveside uninterrupted.

The police chief waited patiently for the villagers to return to their homes before approaching Grandpa Goia. When the last villager turned to go, he hurried to his side.

"Who were the highly decorated military officials flanking you during the funeral?" he asked anxiously.

"What military officials?"

"I am in no mood to play games. Who were the officials and who sent them?" demanded the officer.

All at once Grandpa Goia realized the miracle God had worked in his behalf. Angels dressed as highly decorated military officials had been sent from heaven to accompany him safely through the death squad. A smile came to his face as scripture after scripture promising the protection of heavenly angels came into his mind. With a broadening smile he answered, "My Commander in Chief sent them."

"Well, I want you to know that anytime you want to hold a gathering in my village you just talk to me and I will see to it that you are protected," the officer promised as he turned to walk away.

God not only had protected him from certain death, but also had opened the door to share His goodness to a village where His children didn't know Him. As a result several of the villagers were baptized and started a church.

Pavel smiled as he thought of the courage of those who had gone before him. Sitting alone in a cold stall was not the worst thing that could happen. The disfavor of the military for being a Christian that he was beginning to experience personally was well understood by many who had gone before him.

All day he recited God's promises and praised Him for His faithfulness this far in his life. Each time he heard someone enter the restroom he remained totally silent until he was sure the person was gone. He had never imagined that a restroom stall could be a place of worship, but it most certainly had been this day. He had entered his stall at 7:30 in the morning. Finally at 3:00 in the afternoon he heard the soldiers coming into the restroom to clean up after work. Quietly he slipped out of the stall and back to the barracks. No one noticed, and no one said a word to him.

His first Sabbath had been spent in a most unusual sanctuary, but one filled with God's presence just the same.

CHAPTER 7:

Whatever Your Hand Finds to Do

Eagerly the young soldiers pressed forward trying to find the list containing their name. Pavel was one of the soldiers seeking to discover his assignment for military training. Where would he find his name? He didn't see it listed with the infantry or the mountain hunters. It wasn't on the list for the tank division or marksmen. Continuing to scan the many long lists, he came to the special tactical forces. There was his name under a special force known as Genius. The short explanation stated: This special force will be trained to work behind enemy lines providing booby trapping, land mines, and tactical demolition. "Lord, I don't know how this fits into Your plan," Pavel prayed silently as he walked away. "Help me to trust Your leading one day at a time."

The emergency news bulletin from the Ministry of Agriculture arrived before there was time for the training to begin. Some of the worst flooding ever experienced had left many of the large government farms underwater. It was fall and time for the corn harvest. If the military were not able to harvest the corn, there would be no food the coming year. All training was immediately suspended. Soldiers were organized into groups, to be sent to various farms throughout the country. Pavel's platoon learned they would be shipped to a temporary camp near Bucharest.

When they arrived at the camp beside the farm, their hearts sank. Before them stood hundreds of acres of half-submerged corn waiting to be harvested. The stalks looked as if they were growing from a giant lake. Nothing about this assignment was appealing. They were clearly overwhelmed with the impossible task ahead of them.

The sons of high-ranking military officials, doctors, and university professors were not used to tasks like this. Most of them had never done a day's work in their life. The next morning the camp sounded like a large choir especially adept in the music of grumbling and complaining. As slowly as they could make their feet slide along the ground they shuffled in the general direction of the half-underwater cornfield.

Their new commanding officer was a major lieutenant who took his job quite seriously and wasted no time letting his corn harvesters know it.

Each of the soldiers was positioned in front of a long row of corn. The instructions were simple but daunting: wade down the row picking as much corn as could be carried back to the waiting wheelbarrow at the end of the row. When the wheelbarrow was full, it was to be wheeled to the large farm trailers at the end of the field for unloading. The speech ended by reminding the disgruntled harvesters to make sure they left no corn on the stalk.

It was one of the most miserable jobs Pavel had ever experienced. The standing water had taken on a foul smell in the fall sun. Reaching for corn in the water sent bugs and spiders scurrying in every direction. Occasionally a snake would slither away from their hands as they reached for an ear. It didn't take long for the young soldiers to realize it was easier just to throw the corn at one of their friends than to carry it all the way back to the wheelbarrow. The first 51 rows that were supposed to be harvested was a dismal site. Corn was floating everywhere, with almost none of it reaching a wheelbarrow. Only one of the 51 rows had actually been harvested as directed. The lieutenant was furious as he looked at the disgusting mess.

With angry threats the lieutenant started his harvest team down new rows. Walking directly in front of Pavel, he informed him that he was aware of his absence from work last Saturday. He promised to make him work this Saturday even if he had to walk directly behind him in the cornfield for the entire day. "You will work like everybody else," he declared.

Pavel continued to pray as he diligently picked stalk after stalk. A Bible verse he had learned as a young boy working with his father came back to his mind:

"Whatever your hand finds to do, do it with all your might" (Ecclesiastes 9:10, NASB).

"Lord, help me to do even this work with all my might, even if I'm the only one. Help me work in a way that pleases You," Pavel prayed as he reached for another ear.

Observing his fellow laborers did not make faithfulness any easier. Some of them had slipped away into town and had purchased large quantities of alcohol. Many lay in drunken stupors. These soldiers looked like slumped-over scarecrows sleeping on the few remaining patches of dry ground. Even threats of spending a day in the brig didn't alter their slothful, careless work ethic. Corn could be seen strewn this way and that, with more floating on the water than in the wheelbarrows. But every fifty-first row was picked clean and wheeled to the trailer.

Day after day the story was the same. The endless threatening did not improve the situation in the slightest.

On Thursday a very mystified lieutenant came over to question Pavel. He simply could not understand why Pavel continued faithfully each day while the rest of the soldiers were in a recreation mode. With a puzzled look on his face the lieutenant asked, "Why do you work so hard?"

"Am I not supposed to work hard?"

"Of course you are, but I have checked your rows repeatedly and always find them flawless. You do perfect work even when I'm not checking on you. Why do you do it?"

"I'm not doing my work for you, sir. I always do my work as perfectly as I can to please God."

"I can't believe you," the lieutenant responded with equal disbelief written across his face.

"It doesn't matter if you believe me or not. That's the reason I try to do perfect work," Pavel replied as the lieutenant walked away shaking his head.

That night, sitting behind a large campfire, the lieutenant called his men into formation facing him. Attempting to motivate lazy young soldiers had not been an easy task. He was angry!

"Look at me and listen carefully," he yelled. "Goia! Two steps forward!" commanded the lieutenant. Pavel stepped forward.

"Do you see this soldier? Even if I don't check on him he does his work perfectly. He has a conscience. Most of you probably don't even know what that is! You bunch of spoiled brats, children of generals, sons of royalty, offspring of doctors. You've never worked a day in your life. Do you know what honesty is? Do you know what integrity is? I'm going to see to it that you pay dearly for your no-good, worthless excuse for work. You won't be able to run to your daddy this time. Now get out of here before I beat the tar out of you!" screamed the lieutenant.

Friday morning the lieutenant came up behind Pavel, soliciting his services for a new assignment. "While you're picking your row today, I want you to pay attention to who's working and who's not."

"I can't do that. You will have to find someone else," Pavel replied firmly.

"How dare you tell me what you will and won't do! I'm the one who decides that," the lieutenant replied indignantly.

"I think if you put yourself in my shoes you would understand. You have a family, so you must have a heart. You must know the position that puts me in. I can't be your informer."

After a long pause the lieutenant conceded, "I know; I wouldn't want to do it either. But I want you to know right now that you are not going to get out of your work on Saturday. I intend to see to it that you work your shift like everyone else."

"If you want me to, I will pick two rows at a time for the rest of the harvest. Just don't ask me to work on Saturday."

"I hate your religion, but I do admire you for being so bold and courageous at the same time," the lieutenant said thoughtfully.

Pavel continued to pray for wisdom and courage all day. Each time he saw the lieutenant he repeated his request, but the answer was always the same; his mind was made up.

As he worked he rehearsed many of the stories of God's miraculous leading in the Bible. Almost always the most thrilling stories came from situations just like his: impossible. He resolved to remain faithful whatever the cost.

Friday afternoon as Pavel finished his meal he spotted the lieutenant standing up to leave. Walking over to him, he said, "I have to talk to you."

"No, I'm not going to discuss your foolish religion anymore," he said as he continued to walk in the opposite direction.

Pavel hurried around him, obstructing his escape. "I am going to talk to you tonight. I won't go to sleep until I do."

"Turn around and leave. And that's an order!"

"I'm not going to go. You will have to put me in prison, and if I go to prison, OK, but I'm not leaving until I talk to you."

"Young man, you have lost your mind. You've got to be crazy. We can't talk here where others can hear us. Let's go outside," he said, motioning Pavel to the door.

Stopping in a secluded place, the lieutenant impatiently demanded, "Now, what do you want?"

"I see you are not going to let me off work from the goodness of your heart, so I am going to tell you how it is."

"You are not going to tell me the way it's going to be—that's my job! I'm the one in charge here—not you! I'm not about to start taking orders from some 18-year-old punk kid. Is that clear?"

Just as determined as ever, Pavel resumed his case. "This time *I* will tell *you* the way it's going to be. You have two options: you can leave me alone to follow my convictions and know that you did something good, or you can order me to work. But you know that I'm not going to work, and since your order will be in front of the other soldiers, you will have to put me in prison. Consequently, you will ruin my life forever. In either case, I'm not going to work," Pavel declared determinedly.

"Have you lost your mind? In wartime they would shoot you on the spot for insubordination," yelled the officer.

"Look, you've got a gun. You can shoot me right now, but I'm not going to work tomorrow," Pavel said with resolve while staring the officer directly in the face.

"Are you serious? You would die for your faith?" the officer asked in astonishment.

"I am," Pavel boldly stated. Without pausing, he said, "Listen for a couple minutes longer. I want to tell you a story."

The dumbfounded officer listened as Pavel began his story. "When I was young, we decided to build a church in my hometown. You know that it is against the law to build a church without a permit. You also know that a permit would never be issued to build a church no matter how long you waited. So we decided to proceed without one, building the church at night, in silence."

Seeing that he still had the lieutenant's attention, Pavel continued. "The members divided themselves into groups of 25, working in a rotation schedule. On the night we were to work we arrived a little before 11:00 p.m. so that our eyes would be accustomed to the dark when it was time to begin. We worked through the night until 5:00 the following morning. We used no power tools, hammers, or anything that would cause suspicion. It was slow and tedious, fastening everything with long screws by hand, but after three months most of the walls were up."

The lieutenant stood motionless as Pavel continued his story. "Someone tipped the police about our church building project. The next night they arrived at the locked gate demanding entrance, but they had failed to obtain a search warrant.

"While they were away obtaining the warrant, we encouraged our pastor to escape while he could. We knew we would never see him again if he stayed. Realizing we were right, he quietly slipped away into the darkness.

"In a few moments, with search warrant in hand, the police officers cut the lock to our gate and came rushing in, demanding to know who was in charge of the project. My father stepped forward, identifying himself as the leader. Soon another stepped forward, stating that he was the leader, then another and another. To the frustration of the police, all 25 proclaimed themselves leader of the project. 'How many leaders do you have?' questioned the police officer.

"'We are all equal,' they replied.

"'You are all crazy, just a bunch of fools!' screamed the officer.

"My father was then taken to police headquarters. The mayor, the chief of police, and the chief of the secret service police ushered my father into the interrogation room. For several hours they pounded their fists on the table, screaming that the construction must stop immediately. My father repeatedly refused. With red faces they threatened, 'Then we will bring bulldozers and demolish your walls.'

"My father informed them that there were 270 members, most with families. If bulldozers came in the direction of their church, they would bring their wives and children and stand united in front of the building. If they were going to demolish the building, they would have to run over the bodies of both women and children.

"Becoming angrier by the minute, they screamed, 'Then we will kill you, one by one.'

"'Go ahead. It is better to die for God than to live without Him. If you start killing us, we will go into the markets and begin preaching. We will soon be 2,000 members instead of 270.'

"'You're out of your mind—absolutely crazy,' yelled the officers in a fit of rage.

"'Perhaps in your estimation we are. But the wisdom of God is foolishness to man, and the wisdom of man is foolishness to God,' my father calmly replied.

"The threat of beating and killing the church members did not sway my father in the least. He informed them that the church is the apple of God's eye and that whoever fights against His church is fighting against God.

"Exasperated, the mayor made his closing statement. 'We are not afraid of your make-believe God! When we are finished with you, we will see who is God!' he shouted as he stormed out of the room."

Fastening his eyes on the lieutenant, Pavel ended his story. "On the way home from the police station the mayor and another high-ranking officer were killed in a car accident. They released my father untouched for fear of their own lives. The church members finished the church and built the pastor a parsonage without any interference from the authorities.

"So, you see, if I have to go to prison or die, I will gladly do it. There is a God. And if He allows me to die for His glory, I will do it. So do whatever you choose. Tomorrow I will not work. I'm not trying to deliberately disobey your orders; I respect your authority. I'm willing to die for my country if need be, but I will not break one of God's commandments for anyone."

"I don't know what to say," the officer said very thoughtfully. "If I let you have the day off to worship your God, someone will report me, and I'll lose my job and freedom. What you ask is impossible if I'm to keep my job. But maybe you could not work without my knowledge. Let me think about it," he said as he turned to leave.

The next morning Pavel woke up a little earlier than usual. He wanted to make sure he had God's presence with him before facing the test sure to come. He prayed for the courage and strength to keep him from being intimidated. With peace in his heart he stepped into formation with the other soldiers.

"Each of you line up in front of your row," ordered the lieutenant. Pavel stared back, not moving, as a reminder of their talk the night before.

As the others walked toward their rows, the lieutenant quietly told Pavel to go along with him for a moment or two. Pavel walked quietly to his row.

"Everyone begin," he ordered. Everyone started to work but Pavel; he just stood quietly in front of his row.

Looking directly at Pavel, he repeated his command: "I said everyone."

Pavel knew he was being tested to see if he would really stand for his faith. Every eye turned to watch what would happen next.

As if he had just remembered a previous discussion, the officer asked, "Oh, by the way, Pavel, do you remember what I asked you to do?"

Not quite sure what was coming next, Pavel replied, "I think so, but why don't you remind me?"

"I asked you not to work with the corn today. I want you to catch up my paperwork, remember?"

As Pavel walked to the officers' quarters, he smiled. *The lieutenant just ordered me not to work. Thank You, Father, for an order not to work on Your holy day,* Pavel prayed.

The lieutenant came over to him. "I don't have any paperwork, so just get out of here. If the others see you standing around here, they'll report me. Just get out of here. Go somewhere where you won't be seen, like the forest, and do whatever it is you do with your God.

"I can't believe I just said that," the lieutenant muttered as a very happy soldier slipped away and into the nearby trees.

All day Pavel worshipped his God. He sang his favorite songs with renewed enthusiasm. He had experienced many wonderful church services, but somehow God seemed closer than ever in his forest sanctuary.

A discontented officer's son no doubt made a phone call back to headquarters complaining of the inequity of a lieutenant who had allowed one soldier not to work Saturdays while the rest of them did. Without warning a new commanding officer replaced the lieutenant. His name meant "fox," and interestingly enough, his name and character were nearly a match. He was sly, all right, but it didn't take long to realize that he was greatly lacking in morality. He didn't care about anyone or anything—including his country and the military, only as they benefited him. Pavel could see that reasoning with this "fox" would not be easy. He knew that in just one week he would be right back where he had been a couple of Friday evenings earlier.

Trying to make a good impression on this officer was not an easy task. He definitely wasn't interested in the well-being of any of his men. No doubt whoever had made the call to headquarters for a replacement quickly decided things would have been better the way they had been.

"Get to work, you bunch of oxen! You aren't soldiers. Look at you—you're just a bunch of pack mules! The army doesn't care about you, or you wouldn't be here. You worthless specimens of humanity," screamed the new lieutenant.

What an introduction! thought Pavel. And he wasn't alone. Every other soldier would have gladly traded for the first commanding officer. It would have been humiliating enough to have listened to his initiation speech at the beginning of the day, but it went on and on all day long.

When he thought additional emphasis was in order, he would add an expletive or two. Everything that came out of his mouth was demeaning. All day they endured his constant belittling and harassment.

If any soldiers had hopes of things improving at the end of their day at work, they were mistaken. Commanding them to station themselves by their personal belongings, he began the next phase of his campaign.

"Let me see who has some good food. Whatever you have belongs to me. I want your cookies, your apples and oranges, and whatever else looks good to me." From duffel bag to duffel bag he rummaged, taking anything that pleased him. It was a very deflated group of soldiers who went to sleep that night. Life had just become more miserable than they could have imagined. They desperately hoped the next day would bring some improvement.

The next day the harassment resumed. Things had definitely not improved. Not only were they cursed and called every name imaginable, but an additional amusement was added to their torture. Perhaps in a bad dream the "fox" had decided that he could make life even more miserable for his "oxen" if he would throw things at them as they worked. It was bad enough to watch someone eat your apple, but it was worse having the core come sailing in your direction afterward. For the humiliated soldiers attempting to pick corn, dodging missiles of every sort truly made for a long day.

Thinking that the objects flying in their direction would cease when the food was gone was also a mistake. Surrounded by corn, the officer now picked his own corn just to throw at the rest of them. Now they had to wade through smelly water with bugs and snakes slithering around them as well as having one of the most hateful individuals they had ever encountered as their commanding officer. Pleasing him was simply impossible.

All week Pavel prayed to God that He would help him know what to do for the coming Sabbath. Working out a solution with such an impossible individual appeared hopeless. Friday morning Pavel went to the officer to present his request for a day of rest and worship.

"Sir, I have worked hard all week for you. I have tried to do the best work I could. Tomorrow is my day to worship God." Pavel's request was cut short by a very unsympathetic commanding officer.

"I don't care about your crazy ideas and your day of worship. Turn around and get out of here! Go back to work now!" he demanded.

Pavel stood motionless for a few moments, hoping for an opportunity to explain his position.

"Can't you hear? I said turn around and leave—*now*!"

There was no question that the conversation was over.

All day Pavel talked with God about what he should do. Friday night it took all the courage he could muster to face his new lieutenant. Looking up at Pavel standing before him did not please him in any way. Turning away in disgust, he angrily shouted, "Don't talk to me, soldier. Get out of here."

Calmly Pavel replied, "I'm not going to work tomorrow. If you want to ruin my life, you are free to do so, but I'm not going to work. All my life I've done well in school and I've worked hard at my jobs. But I can't go against my conscience. I would gladly die for my country if need be, but I want you to know that no matter how much it costs me I'm not going to work on the day God says I should rest."

"Yes, you will," he commanded. "Now turn around and leave!" The tone of his voice indicated that he meant business.

The first thoughts that raced through Pavel's mind the next morning were "Lord, help me to be faithful to You no matter what happens."

Calling his men to formation, the lieutenant began his daily intimidation tactics. Without any choice they again endured being called stupid, worthless oxen, as well as a few other choice names. When he was finished, he screamed, "Now get to work."

Pavel stood motionless as the other soldiers walked to their assigned rows. Catching sight of Pavel standing motionless where they had left him, the rest of the young soldiers stopped walking, staring first at Pavel, then at the lieutenant. The lieutenant stared at Pavel with eyes that appeared to be flashing with fire. No one had ever disobeyed one of his orders before, and he was not about to let that happen now.

Looking directly at Pavel, he said, "What are you standing there for? I said get to work!" The stalemate continued, with all eyes waiting to see what would happen next. Pavel calmly stood his ground, waiting for the officer to make the next move.

After a few moments the flustered lieutenant commanded, "Goia, get over here. The rest of you get to work like I told you." Responding to the command, he walked quietly over to see what would happen next. Just as determined as his insubordinate young soldier, the lieutenant continued, "You *are* going to work, and that's an order!"

"No, I'm not. I will gladly suffer for God if I have to, though I hope that I don't have to," he answered respectfully.

"Now I know that either you have lost your mind or you are a complete idiot. Why would you suffer for a God who doesn't even exist? Have you ever seen this God you talk so foolishly about?" questioned the officer.

"No. But I talk to Him every day, and many times I have heard Him speak back to me," Pavel replied.

"Now I know you're stupid, claiming to hear a God talking to you that you admit you've never seen," the officer said as he stared in disbelief.

Attempting to reason with the officer, Pavel said, "Let's think about this for a minute. If there really isn't a God, you will have no problem at the end of your life. On the other hand, if there is a God and you've lived your whole life in defiance of His existence, you'll be in big trouble. But I won't lose either way."

"Oh, yes, you will. You evidently haven't thought about losing your freedom. We will see if you still feel like a winner after spending a few years in prison," snapped the officer.

"Sir, I believe you also are forgetting something. Sooner or later all of us will die. How free will you be?" Pavel replied. Without waiting for a reply he continued, "Let me tell you a story."

"I don't feel like listening to one of your stories. I have heard about all I want to from you," the lieutenant responded impatiently.

"Just tolerate me for a couple more minutes, and I think you will be better able to understand my position.

The lieutenant listened disinterestedly as Pavel retold the story of building his home church. Silently Pavel prayed for God to touch his brazen commanding officer's heart. The story ended once again with the mayor's clenched fist waving madly in the air defying the existence of God.

The officer's face tightened slightly as he listened to the fate of the city official. Trying to appear unmoved by the apparent act of judgment against the mayor, he boldly blurted, "If you think I'm afraid to die, you are mistaken. I'm not. I live for only one pleasure, and that's to make fun of other people, and your little story has not changed anything.

"Well, that may be, but I hope you understand that it's not because of my personal ambition or desire to resist your orders that I cannot work on Saturdays. I just can't, as my conscience won't allow me to."

"You are about the stupidest person I have ever met," replied the officer. After studying the sincerity in Pavel's face for a few moments, he said, "But I'm not going to put you in prison. I don't care about you or your God. I care only about me."

Right before his eyes Pavel watched a hard heart soften. What an amazing transformation! Silently Pavel praised God as the lieutenant continued. "This is the way it will play out. If someone were to report me for not making one of my soldiers work, I would be considered a weak and inferior officer. When the time for my review comes, I would most assuredly be demoted. But this is the way I'm going to work this out for you. When I order the others to go to work, I will assign you the shopping detail in town."

Pavel interrupted. "I hope you understand that I won't do any shopping either. It's God's day."

"You stupid soldier! Just get out of here. Go and do whatever you have to do. Just don't forget to come back at the end of the day," the officer said, shaking his head as he walked away.

Pavel couldn't help singing for joy. Changing this man's heart had no doubt been a more difficult task than holding back the waters of the Red Sea for the children of Israel. His worship began long before reaching the doors to the church. All day he felt the blessing of heaven surrounding him with an atmosphere of peace and happiness. He had just watched God work another mighty miracle.

That evening after he returned to camp the officer continued with his part of the plan. When he was sure most of the soldiers were watching, he called for Pavel to come over to him. "You didn't buy anything. Were all the stores closed today?" he asked loudly. Pavel remained silent as the officer talked on and on, making up his story as he went. His fabrication was a perfect alibi since shortages and empty stores were more common than not. Most of the time there really wasn't anything on the shelves to buy. Consequently stores were closed until something to buy returned to the shelves. After several minutes the officer brought his eloquent discourse to a conclusion with "Perhaps next week the stores will be open for business."

Monday afternoon the lieutenant called Pavel aside and quietly instructed him never to attend church in his military uniform again. Someone had informed the officers at headquarters about a young soldier attending church instead of reporting to duty. Their little plan would surely be found out if he ever returned in uniform again. Having a shared interest in their secret, Pavel assured him that he would be careful not to make that mistake again.

All week Pavel worked with a light heart, knowing he didn't have to worry in the slightest about the following Sabbath. In the hearing of most of the other soldiers he had been commissioned to return to town. Wading through mud and waste-deep water filled with insects and snakes didn't seem half as bad as it had in the beginning. Pavel knew God was blessing him in his desire to put Him first.

As Pavel made his way to town the next Sabbath he knew that it would be his last opportunity to attend church. The month of farmwork had come to an end. Thoughtfully he recounted each of the ways God had blessed him the past four weeks. Not only had he been dismissed from work each Sabbath, but he had been able to attend church and worship with others who loved and served God.

This truly was no small miracle while serving in the communist military in Romania. *I wonder what I will face when I get back to the garrison,* Pavel thought as he made his way back to camp.

CHAPTER 8:

Do You Know the General?

With the corn harvest finished Pavel's platoon packed up to return to the garrison. Returning to the base definitely had its advantages. Camping in the mountains for a weekend with a group of friends was one thing, but a whole month in makeshift barracks was another. Everyone was glad to be back. The next morning each soldier resumed the training that had been interrupted by the agriculture emergency.

I wonder what kind of plan God will have for me surrounded by all these military officials. In just a few days I will be faced with faithfulness to the Sabbath all over again, Pavel thought as he left the barracks. His thoughts were interrupted as he neared his training area. Approaching a group of high-ranking officers, he overheard one say, "What are we going to do? We have to get this repaired, and we don't have much time. The general will be here in a few weeks." Other officers quickly added that they had asked everyone they could think of, and no one knew anyone having woodworking skills.

Respectfully addressing the officers, Pavel inquired about their need of someone with woodworking skills.

One of the officers answered, "The palace that we now use for headquarters is a historical building dating back to the sixteenth century. It used to belong to the ruling king of the day. Many of the furnishings are original and irreplaceable. This morning the major slammed the door a little too hard, and one of the large valances over a window came crashing to the floor. It missed his head by just an inch or two. He could have been killed. What makes it worse is that the valance has to be repaired rather than replaced, because it has the intricate carvings of a famous artist all across it. We need to make the repairs as soon as possible because of the general's inspection in a few weeks. It wouldn't be good for our garrison to be evaluated with the palace in this condition. Now tell us how you might be able to help," he inquired.

"My father is a general contractor and I have many years of woodworking experience. I am sure I would be able to help you with the needed repairs," Pavel said with a smile.

The officers escorted Pavel immediately to the palace to inspect the large wooden valance laying on the floor. Surveying the damaged piece of beautifully carved wood and the window high above them, Pavel confidently explained the tools he would need to repair the valance, as well as the proper scaffolding from which to work in order to reattach it safely above the window. On the spot the relieved officers assigned him the repair project. They assured him he would be provided everything he needed to make the repair.

Being the only one with the skill to do this work is not all that bad, Pavel quickly decided. *I think I could get used to having high-ranking officers complimenting me on my work day after day,* he mused. It wasn't difficult to see that he was receiving a growing respect for his skill and craftsmanship. After completing the repair to the valance, he carefully fastened the heavy wooden masterpiece back over the window, making sure it would never fall down again.

As he was finishing the repair project he noticed the historical weapons display. There were knives, swords, and guns of all sorts. Many of the swords had to be hundreds of years old, and some of the guns dated back to the earliest models ever made. They were neatly organized and displayed on tables covered with beautiful linens. *This is not the best way to preserve these valuable weapons,* Pavel thought to himself.

Calling the major over to one of the displays, Pavel explained to him the problem that would develop with corrosion as a result of prolonged exposure to the atmosphere containing high levels of humidity. The weapons really should be in wooden display cases with glass doors. This way their beauty would be maintained and at the same time would remain highly visible.

"I can see that you would do a beautiful job with the woodworking, but where would we get all the glass custom-cut?" asked the major.

"I have worked with glass many times as well," he assured him. "For some strange reason I even brought my diamond for cutting glass with me, so I could begin right away if you would like," Pavel added.

"I like your idea. Let me discuss your proposal with the other officers," the major said with a smile. After a brief conference the officers agreed that it would be wise to enclose the weapons. Having custom oak cabinets would also be a beautiful improvement for the general's upcoming inspection.

Never had Pavel imagined that he would be building custom oak cabinetry for a palace. How thankful he was that his father had taught him the importance of detailed craftsmanship. Carefully he sanded, stained, and finished each cabinet. When the last piece of glass was in place, the officers were clearly impressed. Examining the finished cases displaying the weapons, they proudly exclaimed, "We couldn't have purchased finer cases from a custom cabinetmaker in the city."

As the officers stood commending Pavel for his excellent work, one of them remembered another project needing attention. Some of the paving stones used for the main entrance had been jarred from their place and needed to be reset. Once again Pavel set out to make the repair as perfectly as he could. When he had finished resetting the stones, it was impossible to tell that a repair had been made. As the officers admired the newly restored entryway they commented, "Young man, you make your country proud. Your skill and work ethic are impeccable." Silently Pavel thanked God for blessing his work in a way that caused him to find favor in the eyes of the highest military officials of the garrison.

Looking first at Pavel, then to the others, one of the commanding officers said with a smile, "I think we are looking at the solution to another one of our problems, gentlemen. You are all well aware of the problem we have been having with stealing in the stockroom. We haven't been able to find an honest man to run the place. Without a doubt we are looking at a young man who has proved he has integrity, and I believe he will prove to be honest as well."

"Goia, we would like you to be in charge of our stockroom." Pavel smiled as he assured the officers that he could be trusted. He knew God was working another miracle for him. The stockroom would give him a place for privacy to worship and pray. In the barracks the constant searches of personal belongings made it impossible for anyone to send him any kind of spiritually encouraging materials. With the key to the stockroom, he would be the one in charge. And he had his own little sanctuary right in the middle of the base.

Faithful to his charge, he kept the military inventory perfectly. Not one item was ever missing. The stockroom's organization and neatness also made a favorable impression. After a couple of inventory audits the officers in charge could see that they no longer had to worry about items vanishing. It was clear they had found the right man for the job. From that time on, Pavel's privacy in the stockroom was never challenged. Dana began to include Bible promises and inspirational quotations in her letters for him to save. Without a Bible or inspirational books, Dana's letters were like a living stream from heaven to his soul.

For a few weeks everything went so smoothly that Pavel scarcely felt like a soldier in the army. Because of the respect he had gained from the officers for his competence in the various projects he had completed, he was treated more like a celebrity than the young draftee he was.

But in a moment his peaceful world was turned upside down. The leading lieutenant of instruction for the garrison scheduled a training event for the coming Saturday that was to include every soldier, with no exceptions for any reason. As Pavel read the posted memo he knew his faith and loyalty to God would be severely tested once again. All week he prayed for strength to stand firm for God. Once again he thought of the courage it had taken for the three Hebrews to stand tall for their faith before a blazing fiery furnace.

"Lord, please give me the courage to honor You just as these young men did so long ago. Help me to stand just as tall for You once again," Pavel prayed as he contemplated the challenge before him.

"Today is the day," Pavel whispered to himself as he opened his eyes in the early-morning darkness. Slipping from his cot, he made his way across the base to the stockroom. No one stirred. They were enjoying their last hour of sleep. Locking himself in his sanctuary, he spent time refreshing his mind with God's promises and prayer. He replayed the many miracles God had already worked for him during his first few weeks in the military. God had been so kind to him this far; surely He had a plan for this day as well. With peace in his heart and God's special presence surrounding him, he walked calmly from the stockroom to meet the day.

Pavel fell into step with the others as they made their way to the training grounds. Falling into formation, the young soldiers found themselves looking into the eyes of one of the hardest-looking commanding officers they had ever encountered. He had come to let them know who was in charge. Calling the soldiers to attention, he wasted no time with formalities or small talk. He had only one item of significance on his agenda. It was Pavel. Positioning himself directly in front of him, he began screaming and yelling with much less dignity than his rank suggested.

"I checked with your other lieutenants. Each of them admitted you have not worked a single Saturday since your arrival at this garrison. Goia, you are either going to work or go to prison. I will make sure of it if it's the last thing I do. Making you work Saturday is going to be the goal of my life. I'm going to make an example of you that will not soon be forgotten. And as you rot in prison I will be promoted to major," the lieutenant screamed like a madman.

The officer's demeanor continued to deteriorate with each determined threat. His whole body began to convulse as he stomped his feet up and down. The young soldiers looked on wide-eyed at the officer as he continued his tirade.

"I'm presently an informer for the secret service police. I intend to make you the object of my next promotion. I plan to work for National Security, and I'm not about to let you stand in my way. You've made a mockery of this country and the military for the last time! Goia! One step forward!" the officer screamed shrilly in tones that made him nearly unintelligible.

Pavel obeyed, taking one step in front of the other soldiers. "Now dig a foxhole," the determined lieutenant ordered.

"Sir, please understand that my conscience will not allow me to work on Saturday. I obeyed your orders to come to the training site with the other soldiers, but I'm not going to participate today. Today belongs to God, and I'm not going to do it," Pavel replied unflinchingly.

"You say, in the presence of all these soldiers as witnesses, that you're not going to obey my orders?" the lieutenant screamed with bulging eyes, which appeared that they would burst at any moment.

"What I'm saying is that it's Saturday and that I'm not going to dig a hole and that I'm not going to participate in training," Pavel replied, standing his ground.

"Disobeying my direct command in peacetime means seven to 14 years in prison, and during war it is 14 years to execution on the spot! Do you still refuse to obey me in front of all these soldiers?" the lieutenant screamed in unimaginable rage.

"Sir, you can make that happen if you choose, but it's Saturday and my conscience will not allow me to work," Pavel calmly stated.

The lieutenant lost all semblance of sanity. He began to foam at the mouth as he shouted, ranted, and raved while leaping wildly into the air. Every soldier stood motionless as he observed the officer's display of rage and insanity.

Leaving the soldiers to themselves, the lieutenant stomped to the palace headquarters more like a spewing volcano than a dignified officer. In a state of shock and afraid to move the soldiers stood motionless for some time, unsure of what they were expected to do. After a few minutes they fell out of formation and began to walk back to the barracks to wait for further orders. Without anyone daring to walk next to the object of the morning's rage, Pavel made his way to the stockroom. Locking himself in the solace of his sanctuary, he prayed as the officers convened an emergency session to decide his fate.

The timing for Pavel's hearing couldn't have been worse, with the general's arrival just moments before the meeting began. Officers could be observed leaving their posts in every part of the garrison to participate in the hearing.

The session began with the lieutenant's dramatic reenactment of the morning's showdown between him and the defiant young soldier. At the end of his graphic portrayal he insisted that the lengthiest prison sentence possible be immediately imposed. With the general present, the presiding officer deferred his position as officiator. Now one of the highest military officials of the nation sat in the seat of judgment. What chance would any young soldier stand against these odds? His doom appeared to be inevitable.

After listening to the charges and a brief discussion, the general requested further details concerning the soldier in question.

"Is he a religious person?" he asked.

"Yes, he is an Adventist," one of the officers replied.

"Is he preaching or passing out religious propaganda to the other men?"

"No, but his example has the same effect."

"Does he drink or get into fights with the other men?"

"No, he doesn't drink and never has had any problems with any of the other soldiers."

"Does he come back from his passes to the city on time?"

"He's always on time and usually returns a little early," another officer responded.

"Then what is he doing that is so intolerable?" demanded the general.

"He refuses to work Saturdays," the lieutenant emphatically accused.

"I have heard all of that, but what else has he done? I would like to know more about who he is before deciding his case," the general continued.

"Do you see all these display cases in the palace museum? He designed and built all of them. He also repaired that valance above the window above you when it fell to the floor a few weeks ago. He is also the one who beautifully repaired the paving stones in the entrance way," another officer explained. "Another consideration worthy of mention would be his responsibilities in the stockroom. Since he has taken charge of it, not one item has been missing," he added.

"And you want to ruin his life?" the general asked in astonishment, looking around the room at the other officers. "I wish all our soldiers were like him. The military is obviously a better institution with his contributions," the general added with irritation in his voice.

Turning to face the accusing lieutenant, he said, with a bit of indignation of his own, "Leave him alone! If you touch this soldier, you will be in direct disregard of my orders, and I guarantee that you will lose your job. If you have nothing more on the agenda, I've heard enough. This case is closed." The general stood and walked deliberately from the room, casting a final piercing glance in the direction of the completely subdued lieutenant.

"Pavel, open the door. It's me," a voice requested from outside the stockroom. Recognizing the voice of an officer who had treated him kindly from the beginning, Pavel opened the door. Looking intently into Pavel's face, the officer said, "Be honest with me. You know Christians are not supposed to lie. You can tell me, and I will keep it a secret. Do you have friends in the government?"

"No, I don't know anyone in the government."

"Are you a friend of the general, then?"

"No; I've never met him," Pavel assured him.

"Well, then, there really is a God after all. The general just ordered every officer in this garrison to leave you alone. This is unheard-of in a Communist country," he said, visibly shaken. Word for word he recounted to Pavel the proceedings that had just taken place. "I would never have believed it had I not seen it with my own eyes," he said as he walked out the door.

Another knock at the door interrupted Pavel's prayers of thanksgiving and praise. It was a sergeant who had also been friendly to him. He began just as the previous officer had, wondering if Pavel had connections in the government or if he was personally acquainted with the general. The sergeant also left with the same conviction: there must indeed be a God.

A loud pounding on the door followed by "Goia! Open the door!" signaled a much less friendly caller. Pavel recognized the voice of the maddened lieutenant. Before the door was completely open, the lieutenant screamed a final threat. "If it's the last thing I do I am going to get you. I'll find something against you before your time is up here—you can count on it." With angry eyes flashing with fire he stormed away, muttering to himself.

From that moment on, every officer on the base knew who Pavel was. They went out of their way to make sure they treated him in a way that would please the general. Perhaps a good word from Pavel would net them a promotion. With a smile his commanding officers told him he was free to go to the city every Saturday, but to make sure he wore civilian clothes to avoid any possible controversy. He was also given a free officer's pass for the train, enabling him to go home for a visit any weekend he desired. The issued pass came also with the hopes he would call the general to let him know how well they had treated his personal friend.

Pavel couldn't help smiling at the providence of God. The other soldiers received only three passes for home leave for the entire nine months, and they had to pay the train fare.

Pavel's reputation as a craftsman netted him many other privileges as well. For his remaining time in the army the officers enlisted his services for needed repairs at their homes off base. He came and went through the gate so frequently that the guards didn't even ask for his ID, simply waving him through.

The fact that God was Pavel's defender was known to all. This general knowledge proved to be very beneficial. Every other soldier in the barracks had repeatedly suffered the theft of personal belongings and special food items sent from home. Because of the fear of retribution from Pavel's God, his things were never touched. It simply was not worth the risk. It was much safer to steal from those without a God.

Truly his nine months in the army were blessed in unimaginable ways. He won the favor of nearly all. Even the madman lieutenant softened over time. Pavel enjoyed freedoms and privileges that were off-limits to even some of the officers. God provided him with his own personal sanctuary. By the time he was ready to return home, his stockroom library housed a considerable volume of spiritual materials sent from Dana.

One MIRACLE After Another

With only a few days of the required service time left, everyone was anxiously counting down the days. Taking the opportunity to go to town for one last phone call, he jumped on the bus, bound for the city.

Slipping his hand into his pocket, Pavel felt for the token that had repeatedly strengthened his faith. Just holding it between his fingers was reassuring. Clasping the tiny coin, he closed his eyes and began to pray, "Father I want to thank You so much for caring about even the little things. You have been so good to me. You have blessed me in ways that I could never have imagined. I know more than ever how much You care about me. You've worked miracle after miracle for me. But right now I want You to know that this tiny coin doesn't feel small at all. It feels like one of Your biggest blessings to me while I've been here in the army. Help me never to forget Your lovingkindness. Long ago You promised me that if I would put You first, You would take care of me. Now I want to thank You with all my heart for the way You have honored Your promise to me."

For several minutes, as the bus bumped along, Pavel silently prayed while clasping the coin at the bottom of his pocket. His silent time of praise and thanksgiving came to an end as the bus screeched to a stop at its destination. Stepping from the bus, he began his familiar walk to the public phone booths just outside the post office.

Taking a little coin from his pocket, he looked at it and smiled. It seemed like just yesterday that he had made his first trip from the military base to the phone booth. The feelings of overwhelming loneliness and his need to hear the voice of encouragement from someone else who believed in God all came back to him. If he could just talk for even a few minutes to someone who understood, he knew it would help him be true to God. Without a doubt, his loyalty was about to be tested.

Remembering his first day at the phone booth, he had searched his pockets for the money he would need to make a long-distance call and was sadly disappointed. All he had was a small coin. He had observed persons making long-distance phone calls place handful after handful of coins into the machine. Comparing that to his one lonely coin, he had concluded that he would be able to say only a quick hello and goodbye, and that would be all.

His smile broadened as he remembered holding his little coin out before God. Looking heavenward, he had prayed earnestly that God would make the tiny token last long enough to strengthen him as he faced conflicts with working on the Sabbath.

Stepping into one of the empty phone booths, he had wondered what God would do. Placing his coin into the machine, he dialed, and waited to see what would happen. After talking for a couple of minutes, he knew that God was working a miracle. The longer he talked, the more excited he became. Hearing encouraging words from home was wonderful, but experiencing the freedom to talk on and on without money was just as wonderful! He knew he was experiencing a wonderful miracle.

After 30 or 40 minutes he had to say goodbye and return to the base. Thanking his family for the courage to be true to God whatever the cost, he hung up the phone. However, the familiar click of an ended call was immediately followed by an unexpected sound. His coin clinked as it dropped back into the change slot below! Pushing open the little door for return change, he stared in wonder at his little coin. God had not only enabled him to talk to his loved ones for a half hour with a single token—He had also returned it for his need in the future!

Pavel couldn't help smiling as he remembered the way he held the coin that day, praising his loving heavenly Father all the way back to the base.

Thinking of all the calls he had made, he was most thankful for the ones to Dana. How their friendship had grown since that day when he was 6 and he had announced his intentions of marrying her. The good news was that Dana had gradually come to enjoy his companionship. As he was preparing to leave for the army she had promised to be his faithful supporter and partner in prayer. Repeatedly she had shared her deep love and confidence in God during their phone calls. Her strong faith had been a real blessing and inspiration. Their absence from each other had truly knit their hearts closer and closer together. The gentle tone of her voice assured him that she would not run from him now. More than one night he had fallen asleep dreaming of the one who had become so dear to his heart. He was now sure he could answer the question Solomon posed in Proverbs:

"A good wife who can find?" (Proverbs 31:10, RSV).

Truly God's coin had confirmed His blessing on their relationship.

Now here he was at the phone booth nine months later to make his final call before returning home. At the end of each call the coin he had used had been returned.

Just as he was about to place it in the slot for the last time he couldn't help remembering the way God had also been able to use it to speak to others. After a few weeks of using his coin he had shared God's miracle with one of his close friends. Convinced that Pavel had fabricated the whole story he had challenged him to prove it. Following him to the bank of phone booths, his friend stationed himself in one next to his. After witnessing a lengthy conversation, he concluded that Pavel had no doubt discovered a faulty phone and had been able to use it repeatedly to his advantage.

"Well, change booths with me," Pavel said, returning the challenge. After changing booths, only to hear his own call ended in less than a minute with the same denomination of coin, his friend decided it must have something to do with Pavel's coin.

"Change coins with me," Pavel challenged again. After they exchanged coins, with similar results, there was nothing for his friend to say but "There really is something to your God."

With memories flooding his mind, Pavel stepped into a vacant phone booth to place his last call. As he deposited the coin and thought about all the times God had faithfully provided lengthy phone calls for him, he felt strong emotions. After several minutes he ended his call to Dana with "I love you and I will see you in a few days." Replacing the receiver, he heard his coin disappear into the machine. The coin box for return change was empty. God knew he wouldn't need it any longer. Walking back to the bus station, Pavel looked up and whispered his prayer in just two words: "Thank You."

Goia **FAMILY** Photo Album

LEFT:
Pavel's parents, Pavel and Eugenia, on their wedding day.

BELOW: 1-year-old Pavel with mother, Eugenia (1965).

Pavel (right), with sisters Ligia (left) and 8-month-old Dani (middle).

LEFT: Pavel, age 3 (1967).

BELOW: Those pockets are full of candy! (1968)

Third grader Pavel plays the violin at the concert hall, Turnu Severin (1973).

Students in the primary school Pavel attended when he was a second grader. He took all his classmates to church one Sabbath. (Pavel is in the front row, first on left.)

LEFT: Pavel, second from right, takes part in a children's program at the Turnu Severin Seventh-day Adventist Church.

RIGHT: The church in Turnu Severin, where Pavel and his wife, Dana, grew up.

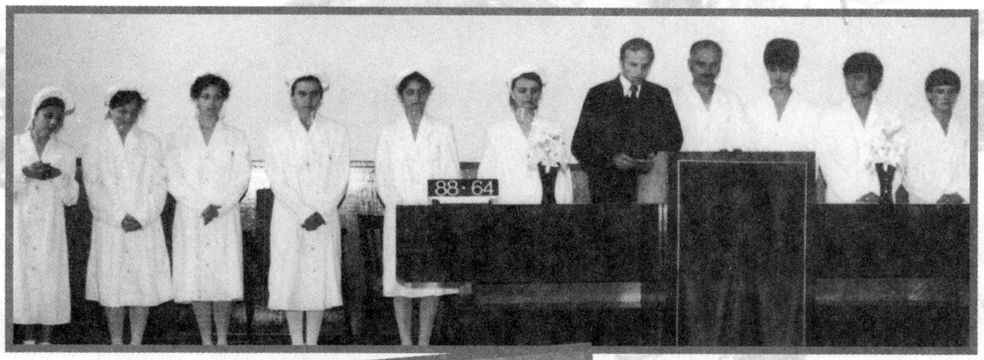

ABOVE: Pastor Emilian Niculescu officiated at Dana's baptism in Turnu Severin in 1982. (She is third from left.)

LEFT: Pavel (first on left) was baptized in 1980 in Turnu Severin by Pastor Traian Aldea (middle).

RIGHT:
Dana, at age 18.

BELOW: With friends from church in Turnu Severin after finishing the new church construction (1981). The police came to close the church and to arrest the members, but God protected them. (Pavel is on the car's hood.)

ABOVE:
In the army
(1982-1983).

BELOW: The museum and the Roman ruins in Turnu Severin, where Pavel and Dana would go to pray and study the Bible together.

Left: Dana and Pavel were married in January 1985.

Below: Pavel and Dana (seated, middle) are surrounded by family and friends at their engagement party. (Pavel's father is in the back row, fourth from the right.)

Left:
Pavel (back row, second from left) sang with the men's choir in the church in Bucharest while he attended Building University.

Right: Members from the same men's choir at their twentieth anniversary reunion. (Pavel is fourth from left.)

ABOVE: A Dacia 1100, like the small "matchbox" car Pavel crashed while transporting a large shipment of Bibles from Bucharest to the towns surrounding his district.

RIGHT: The Ford Taurus the Goias received as a gift from Germany to replace the demolished Dacia 1100.

LEFT: Pavel (front row, middle) celebrates his first baptism as a pastor in Obreja (1990).

RIGHT: Pastors from Banat Conference (1991). Pavel holds poster, front row, left.

LEFT: Graduation day at Southern Adventist University, Collegedale, Tennessee, August 1998.

BELOW: Jack Blanco, Th.D., offers his congratulations.

LEFT: Dana and sons, Gabriel (left) and Ovidiu (middle), share the happy occasion.

LEFT:
A family vacation in Washington, D.C. (2002).

BELOW:
Dana and Pavel on vacation to the East Coast (2006).

CHAPTER 9:

I Will Give Nations for You

"The whistle is probably blowing just about now," Pavel sighed, looking at his watch. The southbound train would be leaving without him. How he had dreamed about this moment. His time in the military had finally come to an end. He should have been experiencing real freedom at this very moment, with the wheels of the train already rolling beneath him. But here he was, confined to his barracks for one more day.

Anxiously looking forward to the end of their term in the military, the soldiers had been checking off the calendar for the past 100 days. With 90 days checked off, they determined each of the last 10 days should be celebrated. As a grand finale the soldiers engaged in one long night of intoxicating revelry. Some of the drunken celebrating had reflected very negatively on the military.

As a final lesson from the military, the colonel decided to punish them by restricting them to their barracks for an extra day. Now, here they sat on their bunks staring at the clock ticking away 24 more hours. No one was allowed a single privilege—not even a phone call home. Their families would no doubt be traveling to the city to greet them as they got off the train. But they wouldn't be there. Instead they were aimlessly shuffling about the barracks.

This isn't fair, Pavel thought to himself. *I had no part in their drunken debauchery and reckless behavior, but I'm being penalized along with those who were guilty.* He knew Dana would be waiting for him. He had called her with the number of the train and the time it would arrive. *What if she thinks I made other plans because I don't care about her anymore?* His tormenting thoughts went from one possibility to another, each adding to his misery. It was one of the longest days of his life.

Early the next morning Pavel and the rebel soldiers were loaded into military transport trucks to be taken to the train station. The commanding officers were taking no chances that they would be embarrassed by another last-minute stunt from these soldiers. They personally escorted them onto the train. At the sound of the whistle they all breathed a sigh of relief. The wheels began to turn beneath them, and they were free at last!

Pavel prayed as the train clicked along the tracks. He couldn't wait to see Dana. She must be wondering why he had not been on the train the day before. If only he could talk to her. As the train wound its way back up the steep Retezat Mountain pass it felt as if it were going slower than ever. The air coming through the window did little to cool him from the hot summer day. Why was this last trip home taking twice as long as all of the others? He just wanted to hurry up and get home and take off his uniform.

Never had Turnu Severin looked so good. From his window he could see the busy city bustling with activity—nothing had changed. As the screeching wheels came to a halt he wasted no time grabbing his bag and jumping from the train. He was on his way home!

"Whew, it's hot," he said, wiping the beads of sweat from his face. Trying to jog with his full duffel bag was hard work with the summer sun beating down on the pavement. Even though he was hot and sticky, the thought of stopping for a rest never entered his mind.

But which route should he take through the city? He had walked at least a dozen different ways from the train station to his home in the past. Deciding on one of the most direct routes, he headed for the city center. Crowds of people overflowed the sidewalks, spilling into the streets. *Every one of the 250,000 men, women, and children in Turnu Severin must have decided to come shopping on the same day,* he thought to himself while trying to navigate his heavy bag amid the jostling crowd. The closer he came to the city center, the more congested it got. Arriving at the marketplace made forward progress nearly impossible. The market occupied four city blocks filled with shops and vendors all trying to entice customers at the same time. The smells from the street vendors' simmering pots were at times overpowering. Most of them did more to repel him than to lure him in for a sample.

As he looked past the sea of humanity in which he was presently engulfed, his eye caught sight of a familiar figure. *This is impossible in the middle of all these people,* he thought. As she stepped out into the street, she saw him. His heart skipped a beat. Walking directly toward him was Dana. *What are the chances of this happening?* he thought. *Just a minute or two earlier or later for either of us, and we would have completely missed each other.*

Spontaneously they leaped forward, running for the long-awaited reunion. With tears of joy running down their cheeks they stood just staring into each other's eyes. Smiling through his tears, Pavel related his countless dreams. Night after night he had pictured her face as he lay on his cot. Dana was even more beautiful than he remembered.

"I'm so glad you still care about me. I thought for sure you had gone home another way to avoid me," Dana said through her tears.

"Care about you? I couldn't imagine my life without you!"

Dana continued, "I wanted to surprise you yesterday with a real welcome home. I came to meet you wearing my new dress and your favorite perfume, and I even baked you some cookies. When you didn't get off the train, I thought maybe you had missed the early train but would be coming on the evening train. But when you didn't get off that one either, I cried all the way home. I felt as if you were avoiding me."

"Oh, Dana, don't ever think those thoughts again," he said, wiping a warm tear from his cheek. They walked and talked for a long time without any real destination. Dana smiled as he recounted the ways her prayers and letters had strengthened him. Many times she had sent exactly the Bible verse or inspirational quotation he had needed to help him with the difficult situation he was facing. God had truly used her to bless him.

Arriving home began another wonderful reunion. The smells coming from the kitchen emanated from something else he had been dreaming about—real food! As his family enjoyed a wonderful meal together, Pavel shared with them the way their prayers had strengthened him while he was in the military. Nothing short of a series of miracles could have allowed him the freedom to worship God week after week while serving in a Communist army. Together they thanked their loving Father in heaven for His many acts of kindness on Pavel's behalf.

After only six weeks' rest from the army it was time to begin his classes at the university in Bucharest. How thankful he was that his father had a good job. Most of the students had to crowd into dormitories. A few of the students coming from families with better incomes rented small apartments, sharing the rent with other students. Pavel was one of the few having an apartment all to himself. Having money for rent, food, and a little to spend besides, he knew he had it a lot better than most. He even had money for taxi rides to and from school. Most students were happy if they had money for bus fare. He felt as if he were set.

However, one major obstacle remained. His classes were scheduled for six days a week. It appeared he was about to revisit the Sabbath challenge he had faced in the military. There were no exceptions or clauses to the attendance policy. A student who missed 16 periods received a warning. In the event that 21 periods were missed, a second warning was issued. After 26 absences, the student was expelled for a semester. If more absences followed, the student was permanently expelled. With classes each day it was not difficult to see that Sabbath observance would be a real problem. After just four weeks he would have 16 absences. There appeared to be no way he could complete a full semester without being expelled. But God had been faithful thus far. He decided he would just have to trust Him one week at a time.

The classes were extremely challenging. All the professors taught as if their class was the only one. He had experienced homework in high school, but it certainly did not compare in any way to this! Each of his textbooks looked more like exhaustive dictionaries than a text for a single subject.

From the first day he diligently applied himself, scoring nearly perfect in every subject. His fellow students and teachers alike respected his aptitude and pleasant spirit in the classroom.

For the entire first semester he attended church without experiencing a problem. When he returned to class after his weekend absence, to his surprise no one said a word. At times the other students told him the teacher had forgotten to take roll. Other times roll would be taken but the professor would forget to turn it in. It seemed nobody else had noticed that the attendance variations occurred only on Saturdays. Because he was such a good student it was assumed he must have been sick or had some other valid reason for missing class. Each morning Pavel thanked God for His faithfulness to him. His providence was making it possible for him to remain in school.

Moving hours away from his home church meant finding another in Bucharest. Soon after joining the church that his friend Pitti attended, Pavel could see that this group's need was the same as that of all the others. They desperately sought printed materials. Only a few had Bibles, and even fewer had lessons with which to participate in the group Bible study. Someone would have to attempt to make copies for the others. It would be risky business. If they were caught, it would mean a lengthy prison sentence.

The government had such tight control on all printed material that a permit was required to own a typewriter. For them to obtain the permit, a typewriter needed to be registered. The type on each of the government typewriters had unique characteristics, making it possible to trace every document. Each typewriter had its own fingerprint, or DNA of sorts. If contraband materials were discovered, the type easily identified its origin. With the constant threat of informers, printing religious materials was extremely dangerous.

From time to time typewriters from other countries could be purchased on the black market. Pavel was told he would be provided a "safe" machine if he would be willing to do the copying for the church. Praying for God to protect him, he agreed to use his apartment as the temporary printshop.

Emptying most of the contents from his largest closet, he soundproofed the door and walls the best he could using pillows and blankets. His closet was now the nerve center of the illegal operation. It was imperative that the sound of typing should not be heard during the night, as the secret service police looked very kindly on tenants who reported such sounds coming from a neighbor's apartment.

His schedule now completely full, he began work in his secret printshop typing out copies of Bible lessons. Typing with eight or nine sheets of carbon paper was much slower than typing with a single sheet of paper. Each depression of a key required very deliberate contact in order for the last copy to be legible. It was tedious work, but without it the congregation had almost nothing in print.

For several months everything went smoothly. His studies were going well, and the people were thrilled to have new materials to study. Many days Pavel fought to stay awake in class. Trying to keep up with his double life allowed for very little sleep. He thanked God as he worked through the long night hours that he could sacrifice his sleep so that others could know Him better. Though he was exhausted, he praised God for the privilege to honor Him.

On his way home from the university one afternoon he saw one of the church leaders approaching him. As he passed him on the sidewalk the leader furtively pressed a small piece of folded paper into his hand. Understanding the system, Pavel continued toward home as if nothing had happened. Once inside the privacy of his apartment, he opened the paper and read the message: "Carbon copies discovered; return machine."

Within a few minutes the printshop closet was dismantled and restored to normal. Very discretely the typewriter was moved back to its owner for hiding. *That was too close,* Pavel thought, returning to his apartment. We'll have to find another way to copy materials. Typing will be out of the question for a long time.

Mingling casually with the other students, he asked, "Where can I find a copy machine?"

"Sorry, the government controls every one of them," they informed him.

With the government controlling the copy machines he would have to try to think of another way to make copies. There *must* be a way.

A few days later his walk was interrupted by the grandeur of one of the city's largest buildings. As an engineering student he began to study the architecture of the massive building. "I wonder what the stress factors are on those load-bearing points," he said as he studied the building. "And what must the dimensions of the foundation be under those giant columns?" his mind continued as he thought back to the blackboard filled with formulas.

His self-appointed assignment as chief engineer of the structure before him was interrupted by a musical voice greeting the guard at the entrance. Glancing over in the direction of the gate, he spotted the source of his interrupted thoughts. A professional-looking woman with a beautiful smile was being admitted through the security gate by the guard. As Pavel turned to walk through the gate his eye caught sight of her name tag.

"You have a pleasant disposition, Maria," he whispered to himself, as if personally addressing her. She continued her pleasant spirit, humming a little tune as she continued her walk toward the building.

"Ministry of Agriculture Building," Pavel read just over the door Maria was about to open. Watching her disappear inside the building, Pavel said, "I wonder if—" Without finishing his sentence, he quickly made his way to the flower shop a couple of doors down.

This time it was Pavel's turn to greet the guard. Presenting himself, composed and in charge, he said with a smile, "I brought these for Maria."

"May I see your ID, please?" the guard asked, disarmed by the moment of romance displayed before him. "Is she waiting for you?"

"Well, look at what I have for her. What do you think?" Pavel replied with a twinkle in his eye.

The guard eyed Pavel steadily for a long moment, then asked, "Do you know how to get to her office?"

Pavel moved his head up and down, and the guard let him in with no more questions.

This time it was Pavel walking up the sidewalk to the large entrance door. "Lord, please be with me," he prayed, not having a clue how he would find Maria once he was inside. *I wonder how many other Marias work in this building,* he thought, looking down the long corridor.

"Where do you think you are going?" questioned a guard, quickly approaching from behind.

"I have come to see Maria."

"Oh, OK. That's her office over there. Knock on the door, and she'll open it."

Pavel knocked on the door, thankful the guard had continued on down the long corridor. The kind woman he had seen a few minutes earlier opened the door with a puzzled look on her face.

Ushering him into her office, she asked, "Who are you?"

"My name is Pavel. I am a university engineering student. Please listen to me for just a minute. What I have come to ask of you is very dangerous. You can either risk your life for those of us who need your help, or you can call the guards and put me and my family behind bars for the rest of our lives."

Totally mystified, she asked, "How on earth did you get in here, anyway?" She could not help smiling as she listened to the drastic maneuver the young man had just pulled to gain an audience with her.

"You are a pretty smart young man," she laughed. "It was nice of you to bring me flowers. That doesn't happen every day. Now tell me what this is all about."

"Our church needs printed materials to use for the weekly Bible study class. You have a copy machine, and I have an original with me. I am hoping you will make copies for us."

All expression left her face. In total silence she stood staring at Pavel, realizing what he was asking. As the personal consequences of the request washed over her, the blood rushed to her face, replacing the ashen color with red.

Realizing what had just been said, she quickly reached for the cushion on her chair. Wrapping it around the phone on her desk, she whispered, "I hope no one has heard us." In quiet but very serious tones she responded, "If I were to do as you ask, I not only would lose my job—I would never see my family again. I'm not willing to risk everything in my life for the copies you need. You don't have to worry, though—I'm not going to put you in jail. Just leave and never mention to anyone that you came here."

"I see you don't trust me," Pavel pressed.

"I don't trust anyone in this country. You never know who is an informer and who isn't. Informers get paid well, and everyone needs money."

"Think about it for a minute. If I risked my life coming here, do you think I would talk when I leave? It wouldn't be just you going to prison, I would go too. I give you my word before God I'll never talk."

"I'm sure you mean what you are saying, but everyone talks if he is beaten long enough. You can be sure they would torture you and beat you to death if they had to. They know how to make people talk."

"I would rather die than talk."

"Oh, I don't know what to do . . . let me think about it."

The next day Pavel returned to her office. Without waiting for her response he handed her the little devotional book *Steps to Christ*. "We also need copies of this book," he said as though she had already agreed.

"I must be crazy, but I am going to try it. You gave me your word before God that you would never say a word about this to anyone, and I don't know why, but I'm going to trust you."

Making a few copies each day to avoid using quantities of paper at any one time, she began. At the end of her shift she took the copies to her home for safekeeping. When Pavel met her at the end of the month, she had a small suitcase full of Bible study lessons and copies of the little book *Steps to Christ*.

Both of them knew that the next step would be equally dangerous. Anyone carrying a suitcase would be suspicious. Without a doubt a suitcase would invite a search. They wrapped the pages in some dirty laundry. Saving the best laundry as "frosting on the cake," they strategically covered the laundry with dirty diapers. Earnestly thanking Maria for risking everything for his congregation, Pavel stepped out into the street, praying that he could make it through the city without being discovered.

Within a couple of blocks he was spotted by the police.

"What do you have in your suitcase, young man?" demanded the police officer. Smiling as if the officer was in for a surprise he offered, "See for yourself." His casual demeanor greatly disarmed the officer as he zipped open the top of the case. "*Phew*! I see what you mean! I've seen enough," he said, closing the case with arms fully extended.

The church members were overjoyed as Pavel distributed the "dirty laundry" among them. They would be studying the Bible from study guides provided by Communist copy machines!

The first semester came to an end with Pavel at the top of each of his classes and the church members rejoicing in the Lord. However, he knew that he would face a whole new set of challenges when his classes resumed. Each class would have a new professor. The grace he had enjoyed the past semester could not be assumed for this one. He was acutely aware that meeting the university attendance policy would simply be impossible if he was true to the Sabbath.

Returning for the new semester, he discovered, to his dismay, that he had been assigned two professors he knew would be exceedingly challenging. One of them had rightfully earned the reputation for being the most difficult to deal with in all the university. As a personal agenda she made it her policy to teach students the real meaning of respect. If she had ever smiled it had not been witnessed. She was hard-nosed and proud of it. Her students would either toe the line or be shipped out, that's all there was to it.

The other noted professor had a reputation with an entirely different motif. Caring very little if his students learned anything or not, he had discovered a way to sweeten his salary significantly. Everything in his class revolved around bribes, or "gifts," as he called them. Students who understood the "gift" system enjoyed unlimited privileges. He had a pleasant personality and a good sense of humor, but the students knew that they had better keep the gifts coming or they would find themselves on the losing side of things.

Both of these unique teachers made it clear that they had a no-nonsense policy when it came to attendance. A student who missed was out. Of course, at least with one of them, a timely "gift" would no doubt solve an absence in one of the classes. With these new professors Pavel could see that it wasn't going to be the same as his previous semester. The attendance would definitely be submitted each day.

All week Pavel prayed for courage and wisdom. He didn't know how God would work it out this time, but he resolved to be faithful. On Sabbath he joyfully joined the morning worship service instead of attempting to please his professors.

Returning to class following the first weekend, he was met by the steel gaze of his hard-nosed professor. Facing him, she went straight to the point. "You missed my class last Saturday. If you do it again, I'll drop you." Her speech finished, she turned and walked back to the front of the classroom. Just seeing the look on her face inspired him to pray all week.

The next period he received another special greeting. The smile on the professor's face helped, but the speech following was not all that encouraging. "You missed my class last Saturday. I think I made myself clear on my attendance policy. However, you still have the opportunity to keep me 'happy,' if you know what I mean. I have been known to be fairly tolerant under the right circumstances," he said, smiling.

After a couple of days without receiving anything from Pavel, he approached him a second time. "You seem to be disregarding my suggestion. Perhaps I need to clarify myself. It's really quite simple. Either you do what it takes to please me, or you will discover a side of me that I guarantee you won't like. If you think you're going to get anywhere in my class without my approval, you're wrong. Let me put it to you like this: as the teacher I hold the knife, and I can slice the bread any way I choose. You had better decide in the future to make me happy."

Pavel responded, "Please listen to me for just a minute. Some of your students come to every one of your classes, but they never learn anything. It seems to me the reason we are in school is to learn. Isn't the whole idea to know the material at the end of the class? I learn even though I miss Saturdays. If you check my grade point average, you'll see I'm a perfect student. What is the big deal if I don't come to class on Saturdays? If I miss something important, the other students gladly share their notes with me. Right now I'm not just caught up in your class; I'm ahead of your assignments."

"You really don't listen well, do you? I don't care if you learn a thing in my class or not. If you don't come with a gift after an absence, you'll be in real trouble. If you miss again next week, you'd better have an extra-special gift. I hope you understand me this time!" His smile was gone. There was no mistaking it—he was serious.

With two professors bearing down on him about his Saturday absences, it was hard to dismiss the subject from his mind. Throughout the week shadowy doubts came from time to time, attempting to steal away his peace. He knew the enemy would love to break his bond of confidence in God. Refusing to entertain the prospects of doom, he increased his time reviewing promises in God's Word. Through his seasons of prayer he drank in fresh doses of courage and power to keep trusting His heavenly Father. Because this experience had become so personal, his devotional life continued to be the most important part of his day. God had not let him down so far, and he was certain there was no reason to stop trusting Him now.

Returning to school after missing another Sabbath was not something he was looking forward to, but after spending an early morning in prayer he felt the familiar peace of God's presence surrounding him. With his head up he made his way back to class. With God by his side he would bravely face whatever came.

Soon after arriving on campus he learned that both of his difficult teachers had met to discuss his absences—that before he had arrived for class they had already met with the dean of the university to report his repeated absences. The dean was known to be even harder to deal with than the two professors. He was a respected member of the Communist Party and had a great deal of power and influence. His loyal support of the government caused anyone having to deal with him to treat him with the utmost respect.

As Pavel entered the dean's office he was greeted by an orderly arrangement of his attendance records on his desk. "Mr. Goia, please have a seat," the dean said, continuing to survey the records. "Upon review of your records from the previous semester I see a highly unusual pattern. I have never seen such a display of incompetence in record-taking at this university. But from the attendance sheets that have been completed I see you have 34 recorded absences," he stated without showing emotion.

Looking up from the attendance records, the dean looked Pavel in the eye. In a polite but dignified manner he continued:. "I know you are an Adventist and that you don't believe in attending school or work on Saturdays. But let me remind you that in this country there is no God. Attending school on Saturdays is not an option—it's policy. There's no way you can continue your education and take off Saturdays. You'll have to choose between education and your religion."

Pausing for a moment to let the real import of his words sink in, he studied Pavel. "These will be your terms for continuing education, not just in our university but for any in the country. This coming Saturday you'll be in your classes. I don't care what you do once you get there; that's up to you. If you want to put your head down and sleep, that's up to you. I don't care if your grades are good or bad—just be in your classes! If you come to class, we will forget this meeting ever took place. If you don't come, you'll be expelled. Consider this your final warning," he said with emphasis.

Making sure his subject was clearly understood, he ended with an ominous promise. "If you cross me, you'll never attend another day of class in your life!"

"Sir, if you will listen for just a moment I think you will better understand my position," Pavel pleaded.

"Just turn around and get out of my office. I have no more time for you. First of all, this God you worship has never been seen by anyone; He doesn't exist. Second, I'm not going to risk my job for you. And last, I think it is stupidity to believe in God. School is more important; it is your future. End of discussion!"

Standing to his feet, he turned and busied himself with a document. Seeing that the possibility for further discussion was out of the question, Pavel stood to make his exit. Leaving the dean's office, he walked in silence. His destiny appeared to be hanging in the balance. If he remained faithful to God, hope for an education would be out of the question.

The next day Pavel went to pay the dean's secretary a visit, hoping he would have an opportunity to explain his position.

"Can I help you?" the secretary asked.

"Is there any way I can get in to see the dean?"

"You must be Pavel Goia. I have heard all about you. As far as getting in to see the dean, you are just wasting your time. Your case is a closed subject in his mind.

"Listen," she continued, "why don't you just come to school this Saturday and pray at your desk? You said that the Bible says not to work on the Sabbath. You wouldn't be working—just worshipping here instead of at church."

"I just couldn't come to school on Saturday without going against my conscience," Pavel earnestly replied. "I'll be going to church this Saturday."

"Well, I guess it's your choice, but it seems a shame that someone with your talent and intellect would throw it all away—and for what?"

Realizing that further discussion was pointless, Pavel left the office. With each passing moment the end of his education appeared to draw nearer.

Night and day he prayed to remain strong and courageous. "Surely God still has a plan. He wouldn't have blessed me all the way through the military only to forget me now," he reassured himself.

The next day Pavel returned to the secretary's office, hoping she would allow him to defend his case. *She seems like a nice woman. Perhaps she will have a little heart and listen to me,* he thought.

Without waiting for her to begin the conversation he began to plead his case. "Why would you be part of ruining my life? I came to school to get a good job. If I get good grades and learn all my lessons, why do you care if I attend on Saturdays?"

"There really isn't any point in discussing this again. I'm afraid it's too late for words. Everything has been decided. As I said before, the only chance you have to get an education is to forget your extremist ideas. Why don't you just admit that you're being a fanatic?"

Leaving the administration office, Pavel returned to his second period class. Meeting him at the door, the professor began, "I told you what to do to keep me happy, and you didn't do it. Now you are going to suffer the consequences. Who do you think is going to save you from the Communist regime, *your God* that doesn't even exist? If there were a good God, He wouldn't mind you getting an education. But it's all irrelevant, since there isn't one."

With the words of administrators and professors alike ringing in his ears, Pavel found it difficult to concentrate in class. For the next two days he spent more time praying than listening to lectures.

During Wednesday night sleep just wouldn't come. Earnestly he began to pray: "Lord, I realize my motivation for coming to this university was pride. I wanted to be someone important with a degree, someone people respect. I wanted the prestige of being able to say that I am an engineer. What is going to happen to my dreams and my future?" On and on through the night he pleaded with God, hoping to convince Him to work in his behalf. The longer he prayed, the more frustrated he felt. It just didn't seem as if God were listening. After increasing the earnestness of his pleadings and not experiencing the peace he was seeking, he ended his prayer. Feeling discouraged and forgotten, he stared for some time into the darkness.

Searching for something to read that would bring relief to his soul, he picked up a small devotional book and began to read a portion he had previously underlined. Scanning the page, his eye caught sight of just the answer he had been seeking. Two or three thoughts seemed to jump off the page at him.

"When we pray we need to trust God with the outcome, we need to allow Him to work as He sees best. We dare not put self at the center of our requests. We should always put God first and let Him decide what is best for us."

Like a flash he suddenly could see. He had been trying to convince God to answer his prayers his way instead of accepting God's will for his life. Realizing the selfishness of his past prayers, he began to pour out his heart again.

"Lord, I'm willing to give up school, my future, and my degree. I don't care anymore. You just work in the way that will bring honor to Your name. I'm choosing Your honor above my wants and desires."

The moment he surrendered his will to God, the peace he had been seeking returned. No longer feeling anxious about the outcome of his education, he fell fast asleep.

The next day as he arrived at the university he was greeted by the secretary. "Have you decided to attend classes this Saturday?" she inquired.

"No, I won't be here," Pavel replied calmly. "But let me tell you about three heroes in the Bible. They were asked to compromise their faith. They wouldn't bow down to the king's statue when the command was given, even though they faced certain death. They could have bowed down with the others, pretending to tie their shoes, but they didn't. They stood tall for God. When the king confronted them, they told him:

" 'Our God is able to save us, but even if He does not, we will not bow down to your statue' [see Daniel 3:17, 18].

"In a fit of rage they were thrown into a fiery furnace. The king stared in amazement seeing them walking around unharmed in the blazing furnace. And when they came out of the fire, they didn't have even a singed hair on their bodies." Looking earnestly into the eyes of the secretary, he said, "God can save me if He chooses, but even if He doesn't, I'm not going to attend class on Saturday. I would rather forfeit my education and future than betray my God."

In disbelief she said, "You have really lost your mind. I admire your courage and determination, but there is no God. What God can save you from a Communist regime? I'm sorry, but there is no one who can save you now."

"It is obvious that you don't know God," Pavel responded sadly. As she turned to walk away, her words of defiance and denial of God's existence continued to ring in his ear.

"Lord, she isn't challenging me now; it's You she is challenging. And I really did mean it when I told her it doesn't matter what happens to me; it isn't that important anymore. But Lord, don't let Your name be dishonored. I know You are able to show her that You are a powerful God and that a proud Communist regime is nothing compared to You."

As Pavel prepared for bed that night he knew his destiny would be decided that Saturday, but he no longer felt anxious for his future. He still felt the gift of peace he experienced the moment he surrendered his plans to God.

Laying his head on his pillow he repeated the words of a favorite psalm:

"In peace I will both lie down and sleep, for You alone, O Lord, make me to dwell in safety" (Psalm 4:8, NASB).

The next morning Pavel began his walk to school knowing that it might be his last. Now he was more curious to see what God would do than fearful of the harsh reality of being expelled forever.

He didn't have long to wait. The secretary of the university was now the one pacing nervously. The moment she spotted him coming up the sidewalk she hurried to meet him. He had never seen her composure so shaken. Her ashen face gave her the appearance of being more dead than alive. Something was definitely wrong.

"Pavel, do you know anyone in the government?" she blurted out.

"No, I don't. Why do you ask?"

Without answering, she continued. "Do you know anyone in the Central Committee?"

"No."

"Then do you know Ceauşescu?"

"No, of course not. How would I know the president?"

"Are you positive you are being honest with me?" she asked earnestly.

"Yes, I am being totally honest. Why do you think I would know anyone in the government?"

Shaking her head in disbelief, she whispered more to herself than to Pavel, "Then there is a God! For 21 years I have worked at this university. Never have I seen the government take an action like this!" She explained: "This morning the university received a mandate from the government with the president's signature canceling all Saturday classes for the entire country, effective today. The letter stated that the government was canceling classes in an attempt to help the ailing economy by conserving energy. If this law would have come on Monday rather than today, you would have been expelled from school for the rest of your life. There is no one who could have saved you. There must be a God after all," she stated breathlessly.

Pavel felt as if he were standing on a cloud as the realization of the amazing miracle God had just worked in his behalf began to sink in. "Let me share one of my favorite promises from the book of Isaiah," Pavel said, seeing a window of opportunity.

"When you pass through the waters, I will be with you. . . . When you walk through the fire, you will not be scorched, nor will the flame burn you. For I am the Lord your God" (Isaiah 43:2, 3, NASB).

Smiling at the secretary, Pavel said, "Over and over I have experienced God keep this promise for me. But now the verse just below these has an altogether new meaning. Listen and see if you don't agree:

"Because you are precious in my sight, . . . and I love you, I give nations in exchange for [you]" (verse 4, NRSV).

Bursting with excitement, Pavel said, "Isn't it amazing? God has given our nation just for me!" The visibly shaken secretary turned abruptly and walked away. There was nothing more to say.

Returning to classes the following Monday, Pavel realized the new law had done nothing to soften the position of his teacher determined to teach him a lesson for failing to play by his "gift" rules. As Pavel entered his class he met him more determined than ever to follow through with his designs. "No gifts, no class, Goia!" Every day he became more incensed by Pavel's presence. His unwillingness to yield to his demands would not be tolerated. His defiance was undermining his authority.

Standing before the entire class, he gave Pavel his final ultimatum. "If you meet me here just one Saturday you can continue in this class, but if you refuse, I am not going to let you take your exams."

After a visit with the dean the teacher was required to admit Pavel into his class. This didn't really help the situation, though. Every test and quiz came back to his desk with an F for a grade. The teacher then announced his decision to terminate his failing student. He was not about to let Pavel off his blacklist. He would soon be gone.

As the dean listened to Pavel's plight he couldn't believe that one of his professors would act in such an unprofessional manner. "This is impossible," he said in disbelief. After reflecting on Pavel's situation, he informed him that the matter was out of his hands and that he would have to file an appeal with the County Educational Commission.

To be examined by the commission meant defending a subject before a board with both oral and written questions. Very few agreed to undergo the process. They would be examined, not only on the subject matter covered in class, but also from any source the examiners chose. Pavel had no other choice. If he was to continue his education, he would have to stand before the commission.

Pavel's scheduled examination day left him just a few weeks to prepare. Going to the library, he checked out every resource he could find. Within weeks he finished textbooks designed as semester courses. Chapter by chapter he prayed his way through each book.

His day of reckoning finally came. Standing before the panel of dignitaries, he was questioned first from one position, then from another. During each question he sensed God blessing his mind with comprehension and clarity, enabling him to answer with confidence. Finally the long, grueling process was over.

The panel of professionals appeared fascinated with the student they had just examined. "You have answered every question perfectly," they assured him. "This commission has not encountered anyone quite like you before. We would like to ask you a final question, not as part of the exam, but out of curiosity to observe your ability to problem-solve. In Bucharest we have been studying a problem with the sewer systems."

After explaining the problem in detail, they asked Pavel how he would rectify it. The answer came to his mind just as the answers in the exam had. Without hesitation he explained the solution to their problem. For a few moments they just stared at him in silence. Finally one of the examiners said, "The two best architects in Bucharest just arrived at the same conclusion after studying the problem for six months. You just gave us the answer immediately!"

The professor refusing Pavel admittance to his classes also had to endure the day in the examining room. After praising Pavel for his excellent answers, the panel turned to the professor for a few questions. He was definitely sitting in the hot seat. When they were finished raking him over the coals, they left little for his imagination to decipher as to how they felt about him as a professor. He left the examination in total humiliation.

Strangely enough, from then on Pavel was admitted to his classes without even a mention of gifts.

CHAPTER 10:

For Better or for Worse

When Pavel completed the first two years of classes, he and Dana decided the time had come to end their long-distance relationship. It would be a bit of a rush fitting a wedding between a semester break, but they didn't mind—they were getting married!

Accepting the offer from his uncle in Turnu Severin to use his spacious home for the wedding reception, the last-minute preparations were made. From now on they would be making the trips from Turnu Severin to Bucharest together.

The day they had been dreaming of for some time finally came. Family and friends coming from far and near, anxious to celebrate the happy day with them, filled the church. As Dana began her measured walk toward Pavel and the pastor, every guest in the crowded building faded from his vision. The beauty of the young woman in the wedding dress walking toward him captivated his full attention. With each approaching step the object of his dreams came closer to becoming a reality. For years he had dreamed of this moment, and now he was living it. With their eyes fixed on each other she approached him standing with the pastor at the front of the church. Extending his hand to hers, his lips sent her a silent "I love you" as his fingers gently caressed her hand.

Dana had finally said yes. She had agreed to marry him. If only she would have seen the wisdom of his plan from the beginning, he would have been spared years of anxious anticipation. Her lack of interest to be his bride in first grade had been the primary object of his consternation. Throughout grade school she had ignored even his most impressive schemes to sweep her off her feet. How she had resisted his flirting for all those years was indeed a mystery.

Now, standing hand in hand before the pastor, both Dana and Pavel knew that their lives were meant to be joined together. It was a beautiful service attended by guests and family from home as well as by many of the friends Pavel had made in Bucharest. In many ways the guest list resembled a choir recital.

With the Communist government slightly relaxing its iron-fist policy against religion, churches had sprung up everywhere. For the past year Pavel had gone from church to church developing choirs. Several had become quite renowned, performing throughout the European continent. In his honor several had come to serenade him and his bride. Without a doubt this wedding had more choir music than any royal family had ever experienced.

The day of feasting and celebrating at his uncle's home finally came to a close with guests wishing them well before leaving for home. The festivities had been more wonderful than they could have imagined. It was truly a day they would remember for the rest of their lives.

There would be no time for a honeymoon for now. They would have to wait for a break in Pavel's classes. He had to be back on campus the next morning. How thankful he was for the nice apartment and the regular monthly budget his father had provided for his education. At least they had a place of their own to call home. Very few enjoyed the luxury of continuing their education without having to worry about finances. They felt truly blessed.

For several months all went well. Pavel continued at the top of his class, and Dana set out to make a bachelor's apartment into a little home, enhanced by the graces of a woman's special touch. Pavel was amazed at the transformation that had taken place. Using a few simple things Dana had changed the drab and ordinary into delicate and enchanting. With each passing day their love for each other, and for God, grew stronger.

Without warning they received bad news from home. Pavel's father had been diagnosed with leukemia, and his illness made it impossible for him to continue his business. Adding to their concern for his health was their realization that without his financial assistance they would have to seriously rearrange their budget. Soon after the news the monthly 2,500 lei they had been receiving decreased to 2,000 lei. The next month only 1,500 lei came. As Mr. Goia's medical expenses increased and the Goia family savings decreased, so did the money they were able to send to Pavel and Dana. It was going to be a real challenge to finish Pavel's last two years at the university. There simply was not enough money to pay for rent and buy food.

It didn't add to their comfort to know that they would soon be parents. Dana was due any day with their first child. How would they meet the needs of their new baby if they weren't even able to care for themselves? They would just have to trust God and do the best they could.

A few weeks later Gabriel was born. They loved the new addition to their family, but things were getting desperate. Each month the decline in income had continued, until they were down to 400 lei per month. They had no food for days on end. This was the hungriest either of them had ever been. Some mornings they lay in bed feeling too weak to get up. Together they would claim God's promises to take care of them.

Often recounting the miracles God had worked for the generation before them gave them strength. Remembering one of his father's favorite experiences, Pavel said, "Dana, let me tell you a story." Lying next to his wife staring at the ceiling, he began.

"You know that our parents' generation lived through a very difficult time under Communism. It cost many of them everything they had to remain faithful to God. But they didn't mind, because their eyes looked forward to another reward—homes waiting in heaven. They lived each day desiring to introduce others to the One who had died in order to offer them eternal life.

"When I was young, my father worked long and hard, carefully saving his money in order to take short leaves of absence from his construction business. With his carefully saved money he purchased Christian books from underground sources to sell to those living in nearby villages. You know how extremely dangerous it was to share or sell religious books. Speaking to the wrong person might mean a lengthy prison term or an 'accidental' death as the result of a beating. But the good news was too good to keep to themselves—they had to share it.

"My father and his friend Bennie often set out as a team on gospel bookselling expeditions. They would quickly make their way through a village just before dark and then slip into the surrounding forests for protection before the alerted authorities had time to follow up on the tip that Christian books were being sold.

"They often walked all night through dense forests in order to be ready to enter another village the following evening. More often than not, their food and money ran out before they were ready to return home. When exhaustion overtook them, they would sleep in the forest as comfortably as they could. Spending the night in the forest with cold and wet clothing was miserable, but they pressed on with the constant desire that just one more person might enjoy eternity as a result of their sacrifice."

Turning his face toward Dana, he continued, "On one of these missions for God, Bennie and my father had tirelessly shared in village after village. It had been several days since they had left home, and they had eaten the last of their food three days earlier. The last of their money had also been spent. Feeling tired, hungry, and joyful all at the same time, they pressed on. It had been worth all the sacrifice as several opportunities had opened before them to speak of Jesus, the one they loved with all their hearts. Both of their backpacks, once filled with books, were now nearly empty. Many searching people would now find meaning for their lives.

"Walking through the forest by moonlight, they recounted the providences of God over their missionary expedition. In order to keep oriented, they walked parallel to the mountain roads. After walking for some distance, they came to a deep mountain gorge. The only way to cross to the other side was a nearby footbridge made of ropes and boards. It was old and rickety, but there was simply no other way to make it to the other side without taking a very long and circuitous alternate route.

"Carefully they scanned the road in both directions for other travelers who might discover them. When they were certain all was clear, they hurried to cross the bridge. As carefully as they could, they walked with their backpacks, trying to maintain the necessary cadence needed to navigate the giant tightrope bridge. They continued to share their experiences as they hurried to reach the other side. My father led the way, with Bennie following close behind."

"In midsentence Bennie cried out, '*Stop*!' My father froze in his tracks. Not daring to move, he slowly turned his head back to Bennie."

"'What's wrong?' he asked anxiously.

"'Look down,' came the faint reply.

"My father looked down at the bridge beneath him. His front foot was resting solidly on one of the cross boards, but his back foot was resting on *nothing*—just air. He was standing on the bridge fully supported, as if all the boards were in place.

"In the moonlight he could see the bottom of the deep mountain gorge far beneath him. With his front foot being the only part of his body supported by the bridge, his heart raced wildly. Ever so carefully he stepped forward to the next board. Turning around, he peered cautiously at the gaping hole created by the missing boards. It was nearly four and a half feet wide. In silence both he and Bennie just stared at the hole in the bridge separating them.

"Bennie now realized he still had to find a way to get across the hole in the bridge. Removing his empty backpack, he tossed it to my father, who was now standing on the other side of the gaping hole. Moving several paces forward to allow a landing area, my father waited with bated breath for Bennie to jump across the hole in the bridge.

"With a mighty leap Bennie flew across the opening, causing the old bridge to sway and bounce wildly in response. When the bridge ceased to bob up and down and weave back and forth, they carefully made their way across to the other side. Once their feet were back on solid ground, they praised God for keeping them from certain death. Together they repeated the words in Psalm 91:

" 'For He will give His angels charge concerning you, to guard you in all your ways. They will bear you up in their hands' " (verses 11, 12, NASB).

"God had indeed sent His angels to place their hands under the feet of His messengers of mercy. My father told me that as long as he lived he would never forget how it felt to stand on angels' hands in the middle of the night suspended over a deep mountain gorge.

"After an hour of walking and talking about the miracle God had just performed for them, they were inspired by their three-day-old hunger pangs to pray another prayer: 'Lord, if You can hold us up with the hands of angels, surely You can help us find some food. We are feeling weak and tired. Please help us find some food so that we will be able to make it to the next village.' Though they couldn't see the answer, they thanked God for His love and watchful care as they walked through the forest.

"All of a sudden my father felt his head thump against a large object dangling by a rope from a branch overhead. Swinging on the rope was a large, round, oven-sized loaf of bread. Once again they praised God for such an abundance of food. The giant loaf of bread was more than enough to fill two very empty stomachs.

"You see, Dana, sometimes we have to wait, but God never forgets us in our hour of need," Pavel said as he ended his story. Together they prayed for strength and wisdom to know what they should do.

Without the money to pay rent, they were forced to move in with a relative. The complicated living arrangements resulted in a very tense situation. After a few weeks, when things became unbearable, some friends came to their rescue, offering them a portion of their home as a shelter until they could find something else. Although thankful, they were still without money to buy food for themselves and little Gabriel. From time to time Pavel went out into the streets collecting cans in order to buy a little milk for their baby. But there was never any money left over for him and Dana. They were desperate.

Remembering the 40 lei he had set aside for tithe from the last 400 lei his family had sent, he decided that they just had to have some food. He would borrow God's 40 lei and pay it back when he received his next 400 lei in the mail. They were desperately hungry—surely God would understand.

The good news was that Mr. Goia appeared to be making real progress in his fight against leukemia. His white blood cell count had returned to almost normal after 10 months of natural treatments. The doctor remained cautiously optimistic, advising him not to resume any strenuous activity until his body regained strength.

However, Mr. Goia had a honey business that couldn't wait for a few more weeks. If he were going to place his beehives for the season, he had to do it now. Loading 85 superhives in a truck, he traveled several hours to the mountains where abundant fields of clover had provided him many years of the finest honey. After unloading the last large hive he lay down in exhaustion to rest for a few minutes on the grass. Nine hours later he awoke wet and cold, and, feeling feverish, he returned home. In his weakened condition he had contracted pneumonia from sleeping on the cold, wet ground. His body had very little strength to fight back after his long battle with leukemia. In five short days his valiant fight for life ended.

His life had been lived as a true champion. He had remained faithful to God in the face of bitter opposition. He now rested in the blessed hope of a soon-returning Savior, his name no doubt listed among the faithful waiting to receive the eternal crown of life.

Returning from the funeral, Pavel and Dana felt as dark and hopeless as at any time they could remember. The move to their friends' house had not turned out any better than it had with relatives. In desperation they accepted the offer to live in the attic of a church member. This would have been bad enough at any time of year, but it was the middle of the summer, and it was *hot*! The attic air was simply stifling, and it was nearly impossible to fall asleep with their clothes sticking to their sweat-soaked bodies. Little Gabriel didn't mind letting them know he was not pleased with their new living arrangement either. What were they going to do? How much longer would they have to live in these impossible conditions?

To add to Pavel's misery, his conscience had not let him forget the money he spent that belonged to God. He had planned to repay it from the money that would come the next month. However, the money hadn't come, nor would it ever be coming. With his father's death came the end of any hope for money from home.

Dark thoughts followed him wherever he went. Surely God must be punishing him for using His money. The little Goia family had come to the end of their rope. The vows they had made on their wedding day had not turned out "for better," but definitely "for *worse*"! It felt as if God had forgotten them.

In the hot, sticky attic Pavel and Dana knelt, asking God to help them know what to do. They reminded Him that He had promised that He would never leave them nor forsake them. They asked Him for the courage to remain true to Him while they waited for His answer. When they finished praying, they agreed they wouldn't tell anyone about their need. Why should they? They had just given it to God.

Entering the church, they were greeted with a warm welcome from Titus, one of the church elders. "Pavel, can I talk to you a minute?"

Curious, they followed Titus to a quiet corner of the church. Looking earnestly at them, the elderly man began. "A few days ago I had a dream. In my dream you came to me crying. When I asked you what you were crying about, you told me you had no place to live." Pausing for a moment to study the faces of the young couple before him, Titus asked, "Is it true? Have you been praying for a place to live?"

"Yes, it's true. We have no money and have been staying in a hot attic for the past few weeks."

"Well, now I know why God gave me that dream. You see, I have a big apartment that's vacant in a nice part of the city. My wife and I lived there until she died a couple of years ago. No one has lived there since. It's completely furnished and is close to one of the city's biggest shopping centers. I think you would be quite comfortable there after you cleaned it up a bit. If you are willing to do the cleaning and pay for your utilities, you may live there for free as long as you are in school. How does that sound?"

A tear of joy ran down Dana's cheek in answer to his question. Together they thanked him for his wonderful offer in answer to their prayers. "I hope you have a nice time at church today," he said with a twinkle in his eye as he turned to enter the sanctuary.

It took very little coaxing for Dana to begin packing their things in the attic. Even though several uninvited creatures had moved into the empty apartment, they had a real home once again.

After a long week of cleaning the apartment was finally spick-and-span. It was wonderful to have a place to live, but they still had no food. Surely God hadn't forgotten about their other need. Realizing He had given a church member a dream in order to provide them a place to live encouraged them to keep trusting Him.

As days turned into weeks with almost no food, they experienced hunger as they had never known it. The few cans Pavel could sell barely kept little Gabriel from starving, but did nothing to relieve the gnawing in their stomachs. Now dizzy spells were setting in as a result of going day after day without eating. They were *starving*! The only way for partial relief was to lie down and hope the dizziness would pass. Something had to happen soon!

Walking home from the university one day, Pavel began to pray, "Please forgive me for using Your money. I promise You that if You help me repay Your money I will never use a penny of tithe money for myself again, even if I die. From this day on, I will be faithful." He continued to pray as he walked the rest of the eight miles from the university to his apartment. He longed for peace with God as much as he longed for food.

Arriving back at the apartment, he found a letter from home waiting for him. Inside was 50 lei. What an answer to prayer—money for food! Feeling hungrier than he had in his life, he remembered the promise he had just made to God. In spite of his extreme hunger he decided to keep his promise. He owed 40 lei from the money he had borrowed previously and 5 lei for tithe from the 50 lei he just received. Taking 45 lei from the envelope, he mailed it to the church treasurer before he had time to be tempted to rationalize a later repayment.

He had just 5 lei left. Together he and Dana walked to the store. They bought a little bread and some yogurt as the two cheapest food items they could find to keep them alive. It was a pretty small bag of groceries, but both of them were glad they had repaid God's money.

A couple of days later as he was walking home from the university Pavel decided to take a little shortcut through one of the city parks. Oblivious to his surroundings, he prayed and cried each weary step of his journey home.

Startled to hear his name called, he turned to see a very elderly man sitting on a park bench. "Pavel, how are you doing?" he asked.

"Oh, I'm fine."

"You don't look fine; you are crying. You don't know me, but I know you. Every week I see you singing in the choir. I'm just a 92-year-old retired lawyer who sits in the congregation enjoying your singing each week. Now tell me where you're going."

"I'm on my way home from the university."

"That's a long way to walk every day! You don't have any money for the bus, do you?"

"It's OK; I don't mind walking."

"You don't look OK; you look miserable. Please, sit down for a minute. I want to talk to you. I have been planning to help someone with my money, and I've been waiting for God to show me someone who really needs it. I believe He just has. This is what I'm going to do for you. I'm going to give you 500 lei each month until you finish school. I also have a very expensive business suit and topcoat I no longer need, and I want you to have them. You may not need them now, but you will this winter," he said with a smile.

Attempting to thank his kind benefactor, he learned one last bit of wisdom. Very solemnly the elderly gentleman said, "You need to remember that when you get some money, always share with others in need. You see, money doesn't really belong to us; we just manage it for God."

Pavel felt as if he had air under his feet the rest of the way home. He knew his bride would agree that things were making a turn toward "for better."

CHAPTER 11:

The Prime Minister's Nephew

It was graduation day. As a result of many diligent hours of study and God's blessing Pavel walked up to receive his degree as an honor student. God had truly blessed him each step of the way. God had not only changed the Saturday classes law for him but had also given him the same keenness of mind in each of his classes as the faithful Hebrews had in Babylon. Pavel had scored the highest of all engineering students. He knew he would never be in such an honorable position if divine providence had not overruled in his behalf.

However, his hopes of beginning a career as an engineer came to an end before they had an opportunity to begin. Even though he graduated at the top of his class, the government considered his religious affiliation a security threat because of the strategic nature of the projects employing engineers.

Disappointed but not defeated, Pavel decided to try residential painting as a career option. Before he really got much paint under his fingernails, however, he knew he was not cut out to be a painter. He would need to explore other options.

Since he had worked as a part-time photographer during his last two years at the university he decided that operating a photo lab might be more to his liking. It was a slow, tedious job developing film by hand. The process required the film to be hand-dipped in just the right solutions for precise time periods in order for the colors to come through bright and clear. But within a short time he became very competitive with other photo labs. In just a few short months he was earning about three times the salary of tradesmen working by the month.

The money was good, but he grew tired of having to shoot weddings and parties. Dealing with inebriated clients was no fun. The night of the party they wanted a photo of everything. The next morning the sobering reality hit them—pictures were expensive. After developing the negatives from an entire evening event, Pavel would be able to sell only a handful. Much time and material were often wasted. Working frequently for free got old in a hurry. He would just have to keep his eyes open for another opportunity.

The conference administrators for the church in Romania began to rely on his leadership skills more and more, and his extensive training in music made him the man of the hour for churches wishing to start choirs. Also, his love for children and their activities made him a natural youth leader. When a camping trip to the mountains or a trip to the Black Sea was in planning, he was called to help with the organization. With the positive response the church received from the youth, he was constantly on call.

The next request for his music leadership came from Caransebeş, a town in western Romania. This church had a lot of musical talent, and so it just needed a little coordinating. For several weeks he traveled west on Friday afternoons to join the church for the weekend. Sunday mornings he made the return trip home. After several weeks of trying to be in two places at once, Pavel and Dana decided it might be best to move the photo business to Caransebeş.

The timing of their move couldn't have been more perfect. Shortly after their move the local pastor transferred to another church. Pavel added lay pastor, youth leader, and evangelist to his previous responsibilities as organizer of the choir. Everything was going well. The church was growing and the photo business was making a nice profit.

There must be a better way to make a living, Pavel thought one morning after coming home from a particularly challenging group of drunken partyers. Inviting Dana to join him, Pavel began praying that if it was His will for them to begin another line of work that God would open another door.

Learning of their frustration, some friends from church encouraged them to consider a business in textiles. They could make a good living in their own home and avoid the frustration of photographing late parties. It sounded like a real improvement to Pavel. "Lord, if this is the business You want us to pursue, please make it clear. If we can't clearly see Your leading, we won't think about it again," they prayed.

If they were going to start a sewing business, the first thing they would need was a large supply of material as inventory. It would definitely require a miracle to purchase material from one of the textile factories in Bucharest. The economy was in crisis. There was a shortage of everything. The shelves in stores were bare. Long lines of people could be seen waiting in the streets hoping a shipment would arrive. In desperate times like these it was usually an impossible dream for new customers to be able to purchase wholesale materials directly from factories.

It wasn't the easiest time of year to walk from factory to factory in Bucharest inquiring about materials. With winter just beginning, rain and sleet would often fall for weeks at a time without a break. Sometimes a little snow would mix with the rain, creating slush. The slush added further discomfort for pedestrians, and that meant nearly everyone. There just wasn't any money to buy a car or even to ride the bus. Walking was the only option for most.

Arriving in Bucharest, Pavel noted the addresses of all 14 textile factories. Walking to the closest one, he entered the business office hoping to negotiate for some material. Locating the office for the sales manager, he went in seeking an appointment. After the manager discovered the reason for his call, Pavel was informed that he was in the wrong department to set up a wholesale account. He would need to make an appointment with the warehouse manager; however, that person was gone for the rest of the day. There was nothing he could do but wait until the following day.

The next morning Pavel arrived early, hoping he could get right in to see the warehouse manager. When the office opened, the secretary informed him that the manager would be tied up for a while. If he wanted to speak with him, he would have to wait a little while until he was free. Pavel's "little" wait turned out to be all morning and part of the afternoon.

After listening to Pavel's request for only a couple of minutes, the warehouse manager also informed him that he had come to the wrong office to set up an account. He would need to see the operations manager. Praying for a patient spirit, Pavel located the office of the operations manager, only to learn that he was not in that day. The manager had a meeting the next morning, but possibly could see him in the afternoon. This was discouraging to say the least, but he had no choice but to wait for the afternoon appointment.

The next afternoon Pavel was ushered into the operation manager's office. After listening to his request, the manager informed him of the shortages throughout the country, making it impossible for the factory to fill its existing orders. There simply wasn't enough material to fill the orders it already had. "I'm sorry—you're going to have to try one of the other factories."

"I just wasted three days only to learn there was no material available," Pavel muttered to himself as he walked along in misty sleet. Bucharest sprawled on and on. It took a lot of space to accommodate its stores, factories, and 2.5 million residents. The fact that the factories were all built in different parts of the city didn't make things any easier.

Tired, wet, and miserable, he arrived at the office of the next factory. The process began all over again. From office to office he trudged, often with long delays in between. After another two-day runaround he was back on the street beginning the two-mile walk to the next factory.

After three long weeks of walking the streets of Bucharest in the rain and sleet, he had been rejected by 13 of the 14 factories. In total discouragement he called Dana to tell her he was coming home. It was useless to waste any more time walking across the city to one more factory that would no doubt treat him the same as each of the others had. Dana encouraged him not to give up without at least trying the last factory. Pavel reluctantly agreed.

With feet scarcely leaving the slushy pavement Pavel shuffled along feeling frustrated that his plan for a new business had been only an impossible dream. Without enough material to go around, a new customer didn't have much of a chance.

By the time he reached the last factory his disposition mirrored the weather outside. He was miserable and wasn't about to pretend otherwise. Finished with wasting time, he went right to the plant supervisor's office. Entering the office, he began the speech he had been rehearsing while walking in the freezing rain for the past two miles.

"I have come to purchase some material for my new sewing business. But I am sure you won't sell me any. Why should you? No one else is willing to sell me any! I have walked through freezing rain and snow for the past three weeks, standing in lines waiting to speak to people, some of whom don't even exist, only to be informed there is no material available. I'm not really in the mood for another runaround from the managers at your factory today. So don't waste my time. Just tell me right now that you aren't going to sell me any material, and I will walk right back out the door the same way I came in."

The startled plant supervisor couldn't help seeing the humor in the picture of the miserable young man standing in front of her with the equally miserable sales pitch. Her smile turned to laughter by the time his speech came to a conclusion.

"Who are you and where are you from?" she asked, still grinning.

"It really doesn't matter, does it? We both know that you aren't going to give me any material, so why do you want to know? I told you before that I wanted to start my own business, but you weren't listening. Nobody ever listens! Why should they listen? They don't really care about anyone but themselves! So I shouldn't be surprised that you weren't listening, should I?"

"Please just calm down for a minute and take a breath. I really am curious where you are from," she said, still smiling and motioning him to sit down.

Ignoring her invitation, he replied, "I am from the south."

"Yes, but where in the south?

"I'm from Turnu Severin."

The lady's eyes widened with interest. "That's where I grew up. I moved away 27 years ago and have not been back since. Tell me how things are going there," she inquired.

Certain his time was being wasted once again, Pavel halfheartedly responded, "Everything is just fine."

"Tell me your name," she persisted.

"My name is Goia."

"Well, how nice to meet you. My name is Goia too! What is your father's name?"

"His name is the same as mine—Pavel."

"How interesting! We are relatives. Your father is my cousin. Now, let's start over again. Why don't you sit down and tell me what you want and what your problem is," she said with a smile. Feeling as though someone was finally listening, Pavel relaxed in the chair he had been offered.

Beginning with his experience at the first factory, he detailed every disappointment he had encountered for the past three weeks. When he finished, she understood perfectly why he was feeling so blue.

"Mr. Goia, this is your lucky day. My boyfriend is the prime minister of Romania. You just stay seated for a minute or two. I think we can have your problem solved in no time," she stated with an air of confidence.

Picking up the phone, she dialed the prime minister's direct line. After she exchanged a few pleasant greetings, the tone in her voice changed. As only a woman in charge of a relationship can, she presented him with a rather pointed ultimatum. "I am sending my nephew over to visit you. If you want to see me tonight, you better take good care of him. If you take good care of him, I will make you one happy man. But if you don't, I will never speak to you again." Clearly motivated, the prime minister instructed her to send Pavel right over to the government building with her driver and he would be waiting for him. After thanking his benefactor, Pavel left with the chauffeur.

The prime minister invited him to sit down and explain his problem. After listening to Pavel's dilemma, he said, "I think we can take care of this without much difficulty."

Picking up his phone, he called the factories one by one, informing them that he was sending his nephew over with a government tractor trailer to select materials from the best of their best. "If you want to keep your job, you will give him whatever he wants. If you don't fully satisfy him, you will be looking for another job tomorrow. Do I make myself clear?" he said in no uncertain terms.

It's amazing what just one phone call can accomplish, Pavel thought, trying not to look too elated. Thanking the prime minister, he joined the government driver as he went back to pay each factory another visit. It was surprising how different his reception was this time. At each factory the managers were waiting for him. They seemed anxious to keep him smiling. He was taken to special places in the warehouse storing the finest materials ready for export. Pavel was ecstatic as he chose from materials that most Romanians had never been able even to look at, let alone to buy. These materials were too valuable to keep inside Romania; they were always sold as exports, and now he was loading a semitrailer full of them. From the response he received at each of the factories Pavel assumed the managers enjoyed their present employment. They sure did all in their power to please the prime minister's "nephew."

After making his final selections at the last warehouse, the big truck was now loaded with almost 57,000 yards of the finest material available anywhere. Feeling humbled by God's providence, he thanked Him repeatedly as they drove along with his precious cargo.

What would Dana think when she saw a government tractor-trailer pull up in their yard? The prime minister had even paid for the 466-mile delivery from Bucharest to Caransebeş. Pavel was more than a little grateful that Dana had insisted he not come home without inquiring at the last factory. He was glad that her faith had remained strong when his had been dampened by a three-week walk in the rain.

Purchasing some used equipment, the Goias were in business once again. From the start they experienced God's blessing. The business rapidly grew, enabling them to hire church members who had lost their jobs for keeping the Sabbath. Pavel now had two full-time jobs. He was managing a thriving business and working as a lay pastor. He seldom needed to worry about what to do in his spare time.

Almost overnight the new sewing business began to boom. The monthly profits were now exceeding 500,000 lei per month. *This is good money in any country's economy,* Pavel thought to himself as he converted the lei to dollars. *Last month's profit was 500,000 lei . . . that's more than $55,000.* God was blessing beyond anything they could ever have imagined.

Just when they thought it couldn't get any better, they received the most lucrative offer of their life. A large firm in Germany had been monitoring the growth of their business as well as the quality of their products. It offered them 2 million lei per month for a merger with their company.

Together the Goia family prayed for God to show them His will concerning the business opportunity waiting for their acceptance. The next morning Pavel got up a little earlier than usual to seek wisdom and guidance from God. He simply couldn't move forward with such an important decision without sensing God's peace. After praying earnestly, he decided to wait until he could see God's leading.

The answer to their prayers came in a most unexpected way. The following evening the ministerial secretary for the local conference called, inviting him to become a full-time pastor. The conference administrators knew it would mean an incredible sacrifice for Pavel to reduce his monthly income from 500,000 lei to 2,600 lei. They knew nothing of the 2 million lei offer waiting for acceptance. Knowing it would be a difficult decision, they simply asked him to pray about it.

Earnestly Pavel and Dana laid their future before the Lord. By the time morning came they both knew that God was calling them to full-time ministry. After accepting the pastoral position, they called the company in Germany to explain the reason for declining its generous offer. They quickly liquidated their business in order to focus their time and talents fully on God's service.

They had one more obstacle to overcome if they were to minister effectively to church members suffering from extreme oppression and poverty. Their parishioners could never relate to them if they continued to live in their plush home filled with the finest furnishings. They also would need to sell their luxury car and drive one of the little matchbox cars that most of the working class were extremely grateful to own. They would need to live just like everyone else. Within a few weeks they had given away nearly everything they owned. Without a thoughtful glance back at what the world had to offer, they moved forward, thankful for the privilege to serve.

Shortly after beginning his pastoral responsibilities the conference office called with a special request. It had been unable to find anyone willing to risk the consequences of transporting a large shipment of Bibles from Bucharest to the towns surrounding Pavel's district. Fully familiar with Bible smuggling from his earlier years, Pavel agreed to the task.

It would be an exciting undertaking with his little matchbox car with gaping holes in the floorboards that allowed water from the road to enter at will. Their family quickly learned to lift their feet when approaching a puddle in the road. The other challenge was space. How many Bibles could his tiny car haul? With a prayer in his heart he set out for Bucharest.

Arriving at the building with stored Bibles, he quickly loaded his little car. With 400 Bibles wrapped in blankets, his suspension was bottomed out. He would be riding on the frame all the way home—no doubt an unpleasant ride. Without stopping to rest, he immediately set out for home. It would be a long night without sleep, but with God's help he would make it.

When his load of Bibles was safely home, he was relieved that he had not been stopped at even one of the many checkpoints along the way. With several hundred Bibles still waiting for delivery in Bucharest, he got back in the driver's seat for another delivery. By the time he arrived at the Bible storehouse, he was exhausted. Once again the little car was loaded to twice its capacity. Again he carefully wrapped blankets around his load of contraband. If he were stopped, he would be in real trouble.

His trip home was much more difficult after driving two days and a night without stopping to rest. His tired eyes were pleading for a couple hours of sleep, but he pressed on, knowing the cover of darkness was his illegal cargo's best friend. After a few hours of driving, his tired body began to shut down, and he began to catch himself sleeping as he drove. Desperately he fought to stay awake.

A few miles farther down the road he opened his eyes to find himself staring at the bumper of a parked semitrailer at the side of the road. He had drifted onto the shoulder of a four-lane highway going more than 80 miles per hour. In a second he would impact the semitrailer directly in front of him, slicing his little car to shreds. Quickly he jerked his steering wheel to the left, and his car careened back onto the highway.

As his car screeched past the back of the semitrailer, his rear fender caught the trailer's bumper, spinning him in circles down the highway. After one complete revolution his car impacted the concrete median, causing pieces of the car to fly in every direction. Repeatedly he encountered the concrete barrier, spinning and bouncing his way along until he finally came to a complete stop. Behind him lay more than 650 feet of twisted metal and broken parts. There was scarcely enough left of his car to recognize what it was.

Climbing out of the mangled mess, he knew he was in real trouble. The police would be at the scene in no time. He dreaded looking into the back seat. He was sure that the Bibles had not survived the repeated impact of the concrete wall. His precious cargo had undoubtedly been strewn all along the highway. But to his amazement, the blankets were still neatly wrapped around the Bibles, without one precious book even falling to the floor. Breathing a sigh of relief, he prayed for God's continued protection.

When the police arrived, they quickly assessed the situation, supposing it had been fatal for whoever had been inside the shredded mass of crumpled metal. In unbelief they looked first at Pavel, then to the remains of his car. In their distraction they completely forgot their routine inspection of the car for contents and called for an auto salvage transport to haul the wreckage from the scene to Pavel's home. Faithfully the officers assisted the roadside crew in loading and securing the car for transport.

Watching from the salvage truck, Pavel mused to himself, *The police are helping me load my car onto the trailer not knowing they are helping to ensure safe delivery of a load of Bibles.* Once they were back on the highway headed for home, he breathed a sigh of relief. He was on his way home—certainly not the way he had planned, but on the way home nonetheless.

Several hours later than expected, Pavel walked through the front door to meet his waiting wife. Without waiting for an explanation, Dana said, "You had an accident, didn't you?"

"How did you know?"

"I couldn't sleep. I had the strongest impression to pray for you. I knew you were exhausted and had somehow been involved in an accident."

"But Dana, we've lost our car. It is a total loss. How am I going to do my visiting and continue my pastoral work without a car?"

"Look at that mess of a car! You should be thankful you weren't killed," Dana reminded him. "And have you forgotten what would have happened if the police had lifted the blankets from the Bibles? The important thing is that you and the Bibles are both here safely."

Dana was right. He was forgetting that the miracle God had just worked in his behalf. After they unloaded the Bibles, he fell into bed for some much-needed sleep.

During the next few days as Pavel prayed, he reminded God that he had sacrificed his car while on a mission for Him. How was he going to continue his work without a car? Without any resources to replace it, he would just be on foot.

A few days later he received a phone call from a woman in Germany urging him to come to her home for a visit. After listening to her unusual request, he assured her that it would be quite unlikely that he would be able to travel. Since he had never been out of the country, he had neither a passport nor a visa to travel to Germany. In most cases it was impossible to obtain these necessary documents. The other problem was his four churches. How could he just hop on a train and vacation in Germany when they needed his help so desperately? The woman understood the obstacles standing in his way, but asked him to pray about it.

Pavel decided that if God wanted him to go to Germany, He would have to open the way. If He didn't, Pavel wouldn't worry about it. He presented his request to the conference administrators, and they agreed to advance him the money for the train ticket and two weeks' vacation with the stipulation he be back in time for the evangelistic series scheduled at his church.

If God was going to open the way for him to go to Germany, a passport would be the first major hurdle. Passports were issued only at a person's place of birth. To apply, he would have to travel several hundred miles to Turnu Severin.

When Pavel arrived at the police headquarters, the officer laughed at his audacious request. He then informed Pavel that it required at least six months just to apply. Pavel understood the system all too well. He had heard of people who had waited more than two years without success.

"I'm aware of all that you say, but I still need a passport," Pavel said, looking earnestly at the officer. "I have 14 days of vacation that began yesterday, so I need it now. Six months from now it will do me no good. If you don't give it to me now, you might as well forget it. I won't be able to use it."

"So how do I know you will come back?"

"You don't. The only thing you have to go on is my word, and I just said I would come back."

"Where do you work?" the officer inquired.

"I am a pastor."

For several minutes the officer sat staring at the young pastor who obviously would not be easily dissuaded. After pondering the situation in silence for some time, the officer asked, "If I don't give you a passport, what will you do?"

"Nothing. I will just go home and go back to work."

"You wouldn't give me a nice gift to convince me to grant your passport?"

"No. If God wants me to go to Germany, I will go. If He doesn't, I won't worry about it."

With a smile the officer said, "You are one crazy pastor."

"So are you going to give me a passport or not? Either I am going to Bucharest for a visa or back to Caransebeş to take care of my churches. Which is it going to be?"

The smile left the officer's face as he walked over to close the door to his office. In whispered tones he made a request of his own. "My wife is a Christian. For many years I have wanted to give her a Bible. Do you have one?"

Opening his briefcase, Pavel took out his personal Bible. "You can give her mine," he offered.

"Go and get your picture taken and come back in an hour," the officer said, reaching for Pavel's forms. Forty minutes later Pavel returned to find his passport ready and waiting. This was truly amazing—in less than an hour God had arranged for the passport he held in his hands, a process that normally took months or even years! His next stop would be Bucharest for a visa.

In Bucharest he waited in another long line at the German embassy.

The lady in charge of registering informed him that he would have to come back in 10 days. "I don't have 10 days. I have a 14-day vacation that began two days ago, which means I have only 12 days left. If I don't get a visa now, I won't be able to use it."

"I'm sorry, but we make no exceptions. The rules are the same for everyone. If you want to register, you will just have to put your name on the list and wait your turn." Reluctantly Pavel walked over to add his name to the long list. As he turned to leave, he heard the woman call to him. "Wait just a minute. I see your name is Goia?"

"Yes."

"Someone from Germany has preregistered you, including all your fees and deposits. If you want to come back in the morning, I will have your visa ready."

The next morning Pavel walked out with a visa in his hand. He knew God was working. It was unheard-of to obtain a passport and visa in only two days. He had agreed to go on this errand only if God opened the way, and He certainly had so far.

Waiting in line for his transit visa through Austria, he prayed, "Lord, I don't believe You want me to be in debt to the conference office for all these travel expenses. Please help me find a way to Germany without having to spend all this borrowed money. You have opened the doors so far, and I know You can find a way for me to get to Germany without paying all this money for the train."

No sooner had he finished praying than an elderly gentleman announced to those waiting in line, "If someone with a driver's license is going to Germany, I will let them drive my car, and I will pay all the expenses."

Approaching the gentleman, Pavel offered to be his driver. Agreeing it would work well for both of them, the gentleman announced he wanted to leave first thing Saturday morning.

"I'm afraid that is going to be a problem. You see, Saturday is the day I worship God, and I don't want to spend the day driving. It really did seem as though it would be good for both of us. I'm sorry it didn't work out," Pavel said with a little disappointment in his voice as he walked back to his place in line.

After a few minutes the same gentleman approached him, offering to rearrange his schedule. "I don't trust any of these people. They may leave me in some dark place in the woods and take my car and my money. But if your convictions are so strong that you won't break your

Sabbath, I'm sure I can trust you. We'll leave first thing Sunday morning."

Driving the gentleman to his destination in Germany, Pavel boarded the train for Frankfurt. As he stepped from the train he found the kind woman waiting for him. Taking him to her home, she invited him to shower and rest for a while. When he was rested, she said, she would take him on a three- or four-day tour of Germany. After they came back, she would tell him the reason for his invitation.

Without even sitting down Pavel responded, "I'm afraid I don't have time for any tours. Please tell me the reason for my trip. If I can help you in any way, I will be glad to do so. If not, I'll just get back on the train to Romania to prepare for our evangelistic crusade."

"You came all this way to Germany. I just wanted you to enjoy it for a few days before rushing off," she said, smiling at his dedication.

"I'm sorry—I just can't spare the time right now," Pavel responded graciously.

"Well then, I might as well tell you the reason I called. God has blessed us tremendously this year. My husband and I each have two cars. Recently I purchased another one. We simply don't need all of them. When I learned you wrecked your car transporting the Bibles we shipped to Romania, I decided you were the one to whom I wanted to give my extra car. So I would like to replace your car and send you home with a few gifts for your family."

Taking him to the Department of Motor Vehicles, they changed the title and registration to his name. Next they purchased an insurance policy enabling him to travel back to Romania. Within a couple of hours the paperwork was complete. Pavel now owned an American-made car that was luxurious compared to his little matchbox car with missing floorboards. With less than 20,000 miles on it, his "new" car really was as good as new.

After one quick day with his kind benefactors Pavel began his long drive home. Almost as soon as he got on the highway he heard a voice urging him to drive faster. The voice came again and again, until he felt as if he were flying. Never had he driven so fast in all his life. He was thankful to be in such a new car traveling at speeds up to 110 miles per hour. Each time he slowed down a little, the voice urged him to speed up. He felt as if he were flying across the European countries.

When he reached the Romanian border, a line of cars longer than he had ever seen were waiting to enter. *What's the reason for all these cars?*

he wondered. Inquiring of another waiting motorist, he learned that Romania had passed a law that day specifying that cars more than 8 years old would not be admitted into the country after midnight tonight. It was 9:00 p.m. In just three hours it would be impossible for him to bring his new car across the border. His car was 8 years and 3 months old.

The voice that had repeatedly urged him to drive faster spoke to him again. *This is the reason you needed to go so fast.*

Calculating the time it was taking for each car to clear the border, he knew he hadn't arrived a minute too soon. At seven minutes until midnight he pulled up to the country line. When his paperwork was complete, he drove slowly ahead while watching the cars behind him waiting to clear. Just two more cars, in lanes on either side of his, were allowed to cross. The officers then closed the gate. The sobbing motorists next in line pleaded in vain to cross into Romania. The law was the law. It was darker than midnight for hundreds of weeping motorists unable to cross the border. As Romanian citizens, their cars were now useless.

The urgency to drive at breakneck speed was gone. The rest of the way home Pavel recounted the ways that God had worked in order for him to be driving home rather than riding the train. Spontaneously his thankful praises rose to God. "Thank You, Father," he whispered over and over. God had certainly never forgotten His promise to take care of him.

Even though it was 4:00 a.m., Pavel couldn't resist surprising Dana. Knocking on the door, he enlisted her help to carry in his things. Rubbing her tired eyes, she asked, "Did you leave your things out in the street?"

"No, they're all in the car," Pavel replied.

With curiosity mounting Dana asked, "Did you borrow someone's car?"

"No, it's ours. This car is a gift to replace the one we lost."

With tears of joy streaming down her face Dana said, "Look at the way God repaid our loss!"

CHAPTER 12:

Mene Mene

The very next morning Pavel couldn't help smiling as he went out to load his new car with evangelistic materials. The spacious car they had received from the kind woman in Germany couldn't have come at a more perfect time. As the beams of morning sunlight sparkled across the car's shiny new paint, they looked like sunbeams from heaven.

The joy he experienced from the dazzling sunbeams was quickly eclipsed by a dark shadow hanging over his churches. A major hindrance had been obstructing church growth for years, and unless a major change took place they would never grow and move forward with God's blessing. The main thing holding his churches back were the church members themselves. It was unfortunate for Pavel, but his congregations were made up of *people.* Though many of them had been church members for years, they were still filled with pride and jealousy. Desiring to have the highest position in church office was not an exclusive problem to the disciples; his members were also doing all in their power to obtain the highest position.

Each of the church elders was sure that his standing with God was far superior to that of the other elders. Consequently, each elder considered himself the only logical choice as the head elder. When one of the others was chosen, the rest of them went behind his back attempting to discredit his leadership. And so it went with each of the church offices. Unfortunately the prideful spirit established by the leaders set a tone of contention for the rest of the members.

Often members engaged in lengthy sessions debating the order of service. One was sure it was more appropriate to call for the offering before the morning prayer, while the one offering the prayer thought the prayer should come first, indignant at the spiritual immaturity evidenced by not realizing that his prayer was most important. After examining the spirituality of their fellow church members, many were confident they alone were being sanctified. Other than the people, Pavel's job as pastor was really not all that difficult.

Pavel decided that God would never bring hurting people from the outside to join his unconverted congregation. Realizing the magnitude of the problem, he knew it would be humanly impossible to bring about unity and harmony. However, he did know what could effect the change. They needed to visit the "upper room."

With Pavel's encouragement they began to meet at each other's homes for seasons of prayer. Kneeling together, they began to realize the true condition of their hearts. As their spiritual eyes were opened they saw only "filthy rags" in place of their supposed "righteousness." The change of spirit they experienced in their small groups motivated them to come together to pray as a church. As a body of believers they entreated the healing power of the Holy Spirit to rule supreme in their personal lives as a blessing to the church. Joyfully the members experienced the love and unity of meeting together as a church in the "upper room."

As a unified body they now set out to share the gospel. Within two years their church membership had doubled. By working with united efforts, they added a new congregation to the district. Energized by the experience, they went into neighboring communities, starting two additional companies of believers. Praying together had truly effected a positive change.

Many of the youth and young adults had become disenchanted with their parents' religion. The kind of Christianity they had observed did not appeal to them, and rather than pretend all was well, they simply quit attending church altogether.

Pavel made it a special point to seek out the missing youth, inviting them to come on camping trips and other outings. After being personally invited several hesitantly agreed. When Pavel shared his personal experiences around the campfire and began organizing them in small groups for prayer and discussion, many of them experienced God's presence for the very first time.

It was not unusual for the phone to ring constantly for a couple of days after a camping trip. Parents wanted to know what Pavel had done to their teenagers. "They're acting so different. They're now praying and reading their Bibles."

Pavel would often respond, "I didn't do anything—but God did."

The Sabbath following a campout usually brought young worshippers back to church as enthusiastic participants. Every time a young person who had been missing for some time came back to church, it became a celebration. Their youthful energy warmed the church in a way nothing else could. Both young and old were thrilled with how well the church was doing.

The government, however, was not doing any better. If it had changed at all, it was for the worse. With the economy really struggling, many of the church members were all too familiar with hunger. There just wasn't enough of anything to go around. Each day was a new test of faith and trust in God.

The shortages included gas for their cars. Long lines around gas stations had become a way of life. Those who wanted to drive would have to wait in line as long as it took. There was no escaping it. Sometimes it meant sleeping in the car for a day or two in the line. Once a car finally reached the pump, 10 gallons was all that could be purchased for the entire month. Gas was so precious that drivers advanced their cars in the waiting line by pushing them rather than wasting the fuel to start them.

With an appointment the following day Pavel knew he would have to make a trip to the gas station just outside of Oțelu Roșu. He could only hope the line wouldn't be more than a day long. Just as he passed the city limit sign he came to a long line of creeping cars. A horse pulling a wagon loaded with firewood plodded along, setting the pace. The winding, two-lane country road had precious few places straight enough for passing, and the line of cars continued to lengthen behind the horse.

As the horse and wagon slowly rounded a bend, a straight stretch of road opened up, providing the weary drivers a long-awaited opportunity to pass. When Pavel reached the wagon, he edged to the center of the road in order get a clear view of oncoming traffic. Two cars and a large truck loaded with construction materials were approaching, but they were still far enough away to ensure safe passing. Taking advantage of the opening, he quickly passed the wagon, accelerating back to normal speed. He was still gaining speed when he met the oncoming traffic. The two cars passed by without incident.

However, when the back bumper of the large truck was even with Pavel's car, a teenage boy, who had apparently been waiting to cross the road, ran out in front of him. With his foot still moving to the brake pedal Pavel watched in horror as the left side of his car struck the boy's hip and leg. He stared out the windshield in disbelief as the impact threw the boy into the air directly into the path of his car. Desperately trying to avoid hitting the boy for a second time, Pavel slammed on the brakes and jerked the steering wheel to the left. His screeching tires skidded to the center of the road. Each second felt like an eternity. The sick feeling in his stomach intensified as he watched the boy's limp body drop in front of the passenger side of his car. It was impossible to avoid him. With a loud thud the right side of his car impacted the boy's head and shoulder, causing him to fly into the air a second time. In anguish he watched as his limp form came down, bouncing along the shoulder of the road. If only this were a nightmare.

Skidding to a stop, Pavel jumped from his car and raced back to the motionless body at the side of the road. He feared the worst as he bent over the crumpled form with blood running from his ears, nose, eyes, and mouth. It was quite clear he was unconscious, but at least he was still breathing. Maybe—just maybe—there was a chance he would live. Pavel felt himself go numb from shock as he looked on in helplessness at the dying boy.

The teenager was known as Mene Mene, so nicknamed because of his severe stuttering problem. Disabled and mentally delayed, he was well known by everyone in the area. He traveled all over town hobbling up and down and sideways all at the same time. He had almost no control of his arms, causing them to flail randomly. He had never been able to play with other kids, and now, though he was 19, it was impossible for him to work. Unable to do anything else, he went around begging, hoping for enough money to buy food. This was not his first time to dart into traffic. He had escaped his previous accidents with minor injuries, but this time his battered body hadn't fared so well.

Another motorist observing the accident stopped to see if he could help. One quick glance said it all. The boy's only chance of survival was an immediate trip to the hospital. With the help of others who had stopped to help, Mene Mene was loaded into the back seat of a nearby vehicle. Thankfully the hospital in Oțelu Roșu was only a short distance away, and within a few minutes the driver transported him to the emergency room. After a brief examination he was transported by ambulance to a larger hospital in Caransebeş better equipped for trauma patients.

Seeing his condition, hospital staff flew into action, administering oxygen and an IV. Then he was rushed to the X-ray department. Several doctors and nurses gathered as the X-rays were attached to the view box for reading. His injuries were so extensive that there wasn't anything that could be done. His brain was hemorrhaging profusely, his spine was fractured in two places, he had a broken hip, arm, and leg, and one lung was severely punctured, explaining the gurgling sounds coming from his mouth. Without warning the pulsing beeps of the heart monitor abruptly changed to a haunting, steady tone. With no blood pressure, his life had ended. Resuscitation was not attempted; he was covered with a sheet until he could be transferred to the morgue.

One by one the doctors and nurses filed from the room. They had done all they could—it just wasn't enough. Pavel remained alone in the room with the motionless figure under the sheet. Kneeling by the side of the bed, he began to pray. *God, what are the people in Oțelu Roșu going to say when they hear that I killed a young man just beginning his life? They know I'm a pastor. What will they think? If need be, I am willing to exchange my life for his. I know You are able to bring him back to life if You choose. I'm asking You—please bring him back. Please, God,* please!

As Pavel was pleading with God, one of the doctors came back into the room. Seeing Pavel kneeling beside the bed, he said, "Pastor, he's dead. Can't you see it's too late for you to pray now? You should have thought of praying while he was still alive. Just go home. We're taking him down to the morgue."

"Do you think I'm praying to someone with human limitations? I'm talking to God. He is the God of miracles. Nothing is impossible for Him. In the Bible He raised several people from the dead," Pavel reminded the doctor.

"I know about those stories. But that was back then. Times have changed. I'm afraid I have bad news for you, Pastor. Since neither of us has seen any dead people walking around lately, you might as well go home. It wasn't your fault, and there was nothing you could have done to avoid it. Just face it—it's over." Ending his consolation, the doctor turned and walked away with Pavel still kneeling beside the bed. After the doctor left the room, Pavel got up from his knees and made his way to the door. Silently praying, he glanced one last time at the lifeless form of the boy under the sheet.

At home it was impossible for him to sleep. Every time he closed his eyes the accident flashed before him. With eyes red and swollen he and Dana cried out to God hour after hour for strength. They were exhausted, but sleep would not come. As they prayed, they realized thankfully that they were not suffering alone. They could feel God's presence as the comforter as He whispered:

"My grace is sufficient for you" (2 Corinthians 12:9, NASB).

Just that morning they had read the words of that verse. They certainly needed His grace at that moment. All night he and Dana continued their tear-stained prayers. Together they pleaded, "Dear God, we aren't trying to tell You what You should do, but we know You're able to restore life. You are the one who created it in the beginning. And Lord, if there is any way You can use restoring this young man's life for Your honor and glory, please do it. If You choose not to restore him, we will learn to live with it, even though it won't be easy. Whatever You see best, we will accept it." As hard as it was, they prayed, "Thy will be done."

The next morning Pavel returned to the hospital hoping to speak to Mene Mene's family. Opening the door to the young victim's room, he found him sitting up in bed, eating! As Pavel's shock turned to pure joy, he saw that he was not the only one to be surprised. A host of doctors, nurses, specialists, and hospital administrators were crowded into Mene Mene's room, comparing two sets of X-rays. On the left were X-rays from the day before; on the right was a new set.

Standing behind the medical staff, Pavel listened to their baffled observations: "The X-ray from yesterday clearly shows massive brain hemorrhaging, but the one from today shows absolutely none. It is easy to see on this first X-ray that the spine is broken in two places, but look at this one—his spine is absolutely perfect!"

"And look at the lungs. We all heard him struggling to breathe, with his lungs full of blood. Now look at them," the doctor said, pointing to the X-rays. "They're normal and healthy. And look at his shoulder and hip over here. They're not just greenstick fractures—they're completely shattered. But once again, they're in perfect condition in this new set of X-rays. The only X-rays comparable are for his arm and leg. They appear to be the same in both. We'll have to put them in casts, but other than that, he appears to be in perfect health."

Over and over they stared at the two sets of X-rays, unable to find a reasonable explanation. None of them had ever seen anything like it. They just couldn't believe their eyes. Unless their X-ray machine was seriously defective, they just couldn't explain a patient being clearly dead the day before and being very much alive and eating his breakfast right beside them at that very moment! With every scientific explanation exhausted, a miracle prompted by the prayers of a pastor was the only option left. Silently the doctor who had scoffed the day before pondered the reality that a dead person would soon be walking the streets.

Pavel smiled as he tried to imagine the mortician arriving for work that morning. He probably had opened the door as he did every day, expecting to begin the normal routine. Perhaps he pinched himself to see if he was dreaming when he saw Mene Mene sitting up on the table. Never before had he been greeted by a cadaver! The previous night he distinctly remembered leaving him wrapped on a table. Now here he was, asking for breakfast!

With eyes needing to be reinserted into their sockets he had stammered into the phone for someone to come down to the morgue and take Mene Mene back upstairs. He no longer qualified as an occupant for one of his stainless-steel tables; he was breathing! Quite possibly he was considering a change in occupations at that very moment.

As the medical specialists turned from looking at the X-rays and began to examine the patient himself, they were confounded by another discovery: Mene Mene now spoke perfectly. Not a hint of stuttering could be detected in his speech. He was without a doubt their most mysterious case.

The doctors put Mene Mene's two remaining broken bones in casts and released him from the hospital. In a few weeks he was ready for his casts to be taken off. When he was able to walk without his crutches, another unexplainable phenomenon became apparent. He had a total transformation in his posture and now had perfect limb control. From that moment on he walked as normally as anyone else.

If they knew God, they wouldn't be surprised, Pavel thought to himself. *Why would He restore him back to life with his previous limitations? His life would have been miserable all over again. Did they think it was harder for God to restore his limbs than to give him back his life?*

Shortly after Mene Mene's accident Pavel went to the grocery store hoping to buy a bottle of cooking oil. He wasn't really surprised when he found the shelves empty. Locating a clerk, he asked her if she knew when they would be receiving another shipment of cooking oil. Studying him for a minute, she called to the back of the store, "Sandy! The Adventist pastor is here. Do we have any cooking oil back there? If we do, you better give him a bottle. You never know; he might pray for your family!" People who had never given God a thought were now beginning to have second thoughts.

Word of Mene Mene's miracle had spread to everyone in the small town. When the evangelistic meetings started a couple of weeks later, the church was packed. Many of the visitors stayed after the meetings, asking for prayer. The response from the meetings was like none any of the members had seen before. When the series ended, the church doubled its membership by those joining through baptism. Together the church members praised God for turning a real tragedy into transformed lives. It wasn't only Mene Mene who had been given another chance to live. Those experiencing new spiritual lives felt incredibly blessed as well.

In the Gospel of John the "Resurrection and the Life" called Lazarus from his dusty tomb with a simple command, and from that day on he walked the streets of Bethany as a living testimony. In very much the same way Mene Mene's restored life declared the Life-giver's power to the people in the small town of Oțelu Roșu. The spring in his step and his perfect stride were irrefutable evidences that His power is still the same today.

CHAPTER 13:

One Day at a Time

Pavel was feeling frustrated. He had been a pastor for several years now, without ever receiving theological training. He didn't like the way it felt when church members asked him questions he couldn't answer. It just didn't seem as if he was meeting the needs of his people or representing God as well as he should. If he were going to continue as a pastor, he felt it would be important to have some theological training.

After praying about it, he sent an application to nearly every seminary in Europe, hoping one of them would help him finish his education. He would have to wait and see which ones responded. As he and Dana talked about it, they agreed that if an invitation did come, they would need some money for travel expenses.

Without having any resources other than their car, they decided to put it up for sale, advertising it in the newspaper. After waiting for some time with no responses, they decided to advertise it at an auto auction. Only one person responded.

As Pavel walked out to the car with the interested buyer he told him how happy they had been with it. As they walked he elaborated the many fine qualities of his car. It had been one of the most mechanically sound cars they had ever owned.

With a smile Pavel put the key into the ignition. After repeated attempts to start the car failed, he gave up in frustration. It just wouldn't start. The man liked the pretty paint job, but it wouldn't do him much good if the engine didn't run. When the man left, both he and Pavel were disgusted.

A few minutes after the prospective buyer left, Pavel went out to try to discover what had gone wrong with his car. This time when he put the key into the ignition the car started on the first try, purring as if it had just returned from having a tune-up. He felt both relieved and angry at the same time. It appeared God didn't want them to sell their car.

After a few months went by without a single university responding to his letters, he felt like giving up in discouragement. He was now thankful their car hadn't started—at least they still had something to drive.

Pavel and Dana decided they were not going to worry about the seminary training any longer. If God wanted Pavel to go to school, it was His problem, not theirs. Putting the whole idea out of their minds, they went back to work for God wholeheartedly.

After another few months Pavel received a phone call from his brother-in-law, who lived in Germany. He encouraged them to sell their car. He had an excellent source for wholesale parts and would be willing to pass on the savings to them if they would purchase a car made in Germany. Pavel graciously declined his suggestion since they had just tried selling their car. It seemed as if it would be a waste of time and money to try again. Why go through the whole discouraging process all over again?

The next day Pavel answered a knock at the door. A stranger introduced himself and asked if he could see the car they were selling.

"I'm sorry, but it isn't for sale anymore. How did you even hear about it, anyway?" Pavel wanted to know.

The man replied, "My wife was getting ready to use an old newspaper to start a fire the other day. Just before lighting it, she glanced down and saw your ad. It was just the kind of car she's always wanted—even the color is her favorite," the man added enthusiastically. "I drove all the way from Timișoara just to buy it. I guess that should tell you how much my wife wants your car. Look, she sent me with cash to make sure there wouldn't be any problem," he said, holding out his hand, bulging with money.

"I'm sorry. It really isn't for sale. We would just have to go out and look for another car if we sold this one. It's been good to us, and we are happy with it. I'm sorry you drove all the way from Timișoara for nothing," Pavel explained to the disappointed man.

That evening Pavel received a totally unexpected phone call. "Hey, Pavel! This is Loren from the United States. How have you been?"

Mystified, Pavel replied, "I don't think I know you, do I?"

"Of course you do! We used to sing in the choir together in

Bucharest. You better remember me—we're related now. I married your cousin."

"Oh, yes, now I remember you. But how did you expect me to remember you after not seeing each other for more than 12 years?" Pavel replied as many warm memories came back to him. "How is everything going for you and your family?"

"Everything has been going well for us here. We own a large construction company that keeps us very busy. But let me tell you the reason I called. My wife and I couldn't sleep a few nights ago. You just kept coming into our minds. We tossed and turned all night. The next day we did a little checking and found out you had become a pastor. We really felt impressed to invite you to come to Tennessee to go to school. I'm making plenty of money and would be glad to cover the cost of your education."

All that he had been taught in school by the Communist government about living in the United States flashed through his mind. He remembered hearing how dangerous it was to live there. People walking down the streets were often shot or stabbed. Women and children were regularly abducted. With most people addicted to drugs, vice was rampant.

"There is no way I would move my family to such a dangerous place," Pavel replied.

Loren laughingly reassured him that it was not at all the way the Communist propaganda had portrayed it.

"Some of those things might be true in the large cities, but we live in the country. We don't even lock our doors at night. In Romania you know what would happen if you left your bicycle unattended in your front yard for even a minute. Here, my bicycle has been sitting in front of my house for years and no one has ever touched it. Let me assure you—your family would be safe. Why don't you just pray about it and see if God is leading you to continue your education here?" his friend suggested.

After Loren's phone call Pavel and Dana realized it must have been God who had inspired the phone call from Germany and sent the man to buy their car. If they were to move to the United Sates, they would need money for travel expenses. They would need to sell their car after all. Now they wished they had written down the name and address of the man who had come to see the car the day before. Without a name, it would be impossible to find him again. He lived in Timișoara, about

75 miles to the west—along with 300,000 other people.

If God wanted them to move to the United States, He would have to open many doors, the first being the sale of their car. Together Pavel and Dana knelt, asking Him to reveal His plan for their lives. "If You want us to sell our car, please bring the man who was interested back again. You know we have no way to contact him. We leave all our plans in Your hands," they prayed.

The next day the man returned, hoping he could get them to reconsider. Returning home without the car of his wife's dreams had not been a pleasant experience, and he knew he wouldn't have a moment's peace unless he came home with the car. "I'll be glad to pay you more than your asking price to make it worth your while, but please, don't ask me to face my wife again without your car," he pleaded.

Without a doubt the trip back to Timișoara would be more enjoyable for the relieved husband this time than it had the day before. He was driving his wife's "dream car" home.

It certainly appeared God was opening the way for Pavel to go to the seminary in America. The transition would not be easy, especially with Gabriel in fourth grade and their newest addition, Ovidiu, in first. Dana was not looking forward to moving again—to say the least. She was quite happy where they were.

Shortly after Loren's phone call they received a letter from Southern Adventist University in Collegedale, Tennessee. The letter stated that Pavel had been accepted as a student for the coming semester beginning in August. At the end of the letter was the promise found in Jeremiah 29:11.

If God was really leading them to Tennessee it would require a trip to the American embassy for visas. If they would be some of the fortunate few to actually get them, they knew it would be nothing short of a miracle. Almost everyone attempting to get one returned in bitter disappointment.

With an appointment scheduled, the Goia family borrowed a car from a good friend at church and set out for Bucharest. As they drove along, Dana further clarified her position. She was not in favor of moving to a country in which they had no friends or family and did not speak the language. She made sure Pavel knew she was praying that their visas would be denied.

Arriving at the embassy late at night, they parked nearby and slept for a few hours. At 3:00 the next morning Pavel opened his daily devotional book to spend a few moments with God before beginning his long wait in line to apply for visas. Opening to the page for the day he discovered that the Scripture text was Jeremiah 29:11, the same passage of promise as on his acceptance letter. Was this a coincidence, or was God trying to tell him something? He would soon see.

Getting out of the car, he joined the others waiting in the four-abreast line that was already beginning to snake around the block. Apparently the ones at the beginning of the line had been standing there *all night.* Registering just after 3:00 in the morning, he became number 956.

Waiting hour after hour in the long line, he watched people repeatedly exit the embassy with disappointed hopes and dashed dreams. Many wept bitterly when the privilege of visiting a friend or relative in the United Sates was denied. Of the hundreds of people applying for a visa, he had seen only four or five leave with smiles on their faces. It appeared that it wouldn't be all that difficult for God to answer Dana's prayer for the denial of their visas.

It was almost noon before his turn came to speak to a representative. Stepping up to his assigned booth, he introduced himself to the waiting official.

"Why do you want to go to the United Sates?" the consul coldly began.

"I want to go to school," Pavel answered calmly.

"You must know that there are schools in Romania. Why don't you go to one of them?"

"I know we have schools here, but they aren't accredited. I want to attend a seminary that will help me be the best pastor I can be," Pavel informed him.

"You're just like everyone else. You just want to go and try to make a lot of money," the official retorted sternly.

"No, that's not true. I gave up a lot of money to become a pastor. Money has nothing to do with it."

"Can you prove that?"

"Sure; you can easily verify my previous business."

"If I were to give you a visa, how do I know you would come back?"

"You don't."

"Then I can't give you a visa."

"That's OK with me," Pavel said, turning to walk away.

"Wait! Come back here a minute," the consul called. "Aren't you sorry you won't be able to go to school?"

"No. Attending the seminary is not up to me. Because I've given it to God in prayer, it's entirely up to Him. I'm not begging to go. It would be much easier to stay here. If I go, I would have to start life all over again, even learning a new language. So if God wants me to go, I will go. If not, I will stay. If He wants me to go to some remote part of Africa, I will go. If He wants me to go to war-torn Yugoslavia, I will go."

"Well, if I let you go alone, you would be able to go to school, and we wouldn't have to worry about you coming back when you were finished. How does that sound to you?" the official offered as a compromise.

"Sir, do you have a family?" Pavel asked earnestly.

"Yes, I do."

"Would you leave them and go to another country for several years?"

"No, I guess I wouldn't," the official admitted.

"Well, neither will I. If all of us can't go together, I'm not going at all."

"Then I'm afraid I can't let you go," the official replied in frustration.

"As I said before, it really doesn't matter to me either way."

"Then you will never get to see America."

"I don't care. That was never my reason for wanting to go anyway," Pavel responded disinterestedly.

"If I were to give your family visas, would you promise me you would come back?"

"No," Pavel answered to the bewildered official.

"Then I can't give your family visas."

"That's OK. I don't care. You see, if God wants me to come back, I will come back. If He wants me to stay, I will stay. But until I know what God wants me to do, I can't promise anyone," Pavel explained.

"You're one crazy pastor," the mystified consul replied. Then he just stared in silence for several minutes before saying, "I'm going to give you and your family their visas."

After collecting his documents Pavel left the embassy not knowing whether he should be happy or sad. Realizing he had just become one of the few out of nearly 1,000 applicants to get a visa, he knew a move to the United States had to be part of God's plan. He also was quite sure he knew a person who wouldn't be rejoicing. All her pleading had not altered God's plan for their family.

When Pavel showed Dana their visas, one for each member of the family, she couldn't believe it. She also had witnessed the number of people who were being turned away. The odds of Pavel returning with visas were so slim that she hadn't really been too concerned, although she did continue her wishful prayers. When Pavel returned with the documents in hand, it was clear that she and God had had different plans.

After again giving away everything they owned, they set out for the airport. Already Dana was feeling homesick. But in spite of her feelings, she too wanted to follow God wherever He was leading. The little family boarded the plane. Destination: Collegedale, Tennessee, and the United States of America.

Loren helped them find an apartment and register for school, paying all their expenses for the first two months. When their bills came due again, Loren called to let them know he would be leaving town for a couple of days. He was going to collect a final payment on a large construction project one of his crews had just finished. When he came back, he would pay their expenses for the rest of the year as a matter of convenience to both of them.

A day or two later Pavel and Dana received a phone call informing them that Loren had gone into cardiac arrest while on his business trip. After assessing his condition, doctors quickily determined that he was suffering an acute case of amnesia. Loren didn't even know who his wife was, let alone Pavel and Dana. Without medical insurance, Loren had accumulated such enormous medical bills that it wouldn't have mattered if he did remember them.

Now they were alone in a strange country, with no friends. They didn't know the language and had very little food remaining on their shelves. And to make matters worse, their rent was due. They felt more helpless and alone than at any time they could remember.

In tears Dana cried out in prayer, "Dear God, You know we weren't the ones asking to come here, and I even prayed we wouldn't. But You worked miracle after miracle to bring us here. Why would You let this happen? Surely it wasn't Your plan to bring us here and then let us starve to death." Having given their plight to God, they decided they wouldn't tell anyone of their dire need. God understood it all. He surely had a solution to their dilemma.

The next day, while walking across campus, Pavel decided to talk to God about his need at a special place known as the Prayer Garden. Leaning up against a large maple tree, he prayed as the tears ran down his cheeks. "Lord, I know You brought us here. Please don't forsake us now."

A firm pat on the back interrupted his tearful prayer. It was the dean of the seminary. "What's wrong, Pavel? It looks as though things aren't going so well."

In the few English words he knew, Pavel replied, "We are facing some challenges, just as all students do, and I have been asking God for help."

"Please come to my office. I want to hear more of your story," the dean urged.

Arriving at his office, Pavel explained all of the unfortunate circumstances that had just taken place. They didn't know what to do next. "We aren't asking for anything from anyone, but you asked, and now you know a little of what we are facing. We just don't know what to do next."

"Well, if God brought you here, surely He will provide for your needs. I'm sure you must know that by now," the dean reminded him.

The next Sabbath the campus pastor preached his sermon from Jeremiah 29:11:

"I know the plans that I have for you . . ." (NASB).

The words of encouragement from this passage were just what Pavel and Dana needed to hear. Leaning over to her, he whispered, "Dana, he's preaching from our verse." They listened attentively as the pastor detailed many of the challenges that Moses faced as God called him to lead the Israelites out of Egypt. It wasn't Moses' ability that God needed as much as his availability. It wasn't what Moses held in his hand that made the difference; it was what God could do with it. Continuing his message, the pastor reminded the congregation how inadequate Moses felt when God's plan included going to a country in which he couldn't even speak the language. Facing each other in the pew, Pavel and Dana both knew that God was speaking directly to them. While sitting in the pew with tears rolling down their cheeks, they asked God to forgive them for ever doubting Him. Once again they resolved to trust Him for all their needs.

Shaking hands with the pastor on the way out of the sanctuary, they thanked him for allowing God to use him to speak words that were just for them.

"Who are you?" the smiling pastor inquired.

"We are students at the seminary from Romania," they said as they thanked him again.

The apartment shelves were still bare, but the dark cloud that had followed them to church that morning had vanished. In God's presence the sunlight of heaven had broken through. Their circumstances had not changed, but they were God's children, and they knew He would take care of them.

The following Thursday evening Pavel responded to a knock at the door. It was the pastor. He wondered if he could come in to talk to them for a few minutes. He informed them the dean had already shared part of their story with him, and he wanted to hear the rest of it.

When they finished detailing their situation, the pastor told them that the dean had already offered to pay all of Pavel's tuition for the year, but on one condition. He had to finish his two-year course in one year and still maintain an excellent grade point average. The pastor then said he would talk to the church about paying their housing and insurance. They would have to pay for their food, utilities, and Pavel's textbooks on their own.

Dana soon found three homes to clean, in addition to caring for an older woman during the day and an elderly man at night. With Pavel tuning a few pianos they managed to barely scrape by.

In order to finish his classes in one year Pavel had to take 21 credits the first semester and 19 the second, followed by 17 in the summer. In his "spare time," he had to learn English and take a computer class. He felt equally lost in both classes, not knowing even how to turn on a computer.

He spent many nights praying by his bed with a dictionary in hand while trying to figure out how to type using all foreign characters on the keyboard. His assignments usually took him until about 3:00 in the morning to complete. With only an hour's sleep he'd get up in order to have time to pray before starting the new day. His schedule was unbelievable, but he made it through with God's help. When the school year was finished, Pavel graduated magna cum laude.

With only a few weeks remaining until graduation, the dean of the seminary approached Pavel with the same offer of sponsorship for his Master of Divinity degree. If he could complete his master's degree at

Andrews University in Berrien Springs, Michigan, in half the time, while maintaining his same grade point average, he would again pay the tuition.

Only two weeks remained until the fall semester at Andrews University was to begin. He had no money, and no way to move his family. And they had to move out of the student housing that had been their residence. Once again they couldn't move forward, and they couldn't stay where they were.

Learning of their predicament, the son of the retired man that Dana was caring for came to the rescue. Again and again he had helped them through emergencies. The entire Goia family was extremely grateful for this kind man who had repeatedly shared his time and means. He had made them feel as if they were members of his own family. As family members, he invited them to move in with him until they decided what they were going to do.

Even though they were not sure how they would ever make the move to Andrews University or where they would live once they were there, the dean registered Pavel and paid his tuition. Pavel called the student housing department repeatedly, hoping an apartment had become available, but everything was still full. With only two days until classes were to begin, it appeared that the move would be impossible. Even if they could find a way to get there, they wouldn't have a place to live.

Later that day a truck driver called the house where the Goia family was staying to make sure someone was there. He had a table to deliver from an aunt in Florida. She had asked the driver to deliver it since their home wouldn't be too far out of his way. From there he would be driving to Andrews University with a load of furniture for a student.

After the driver unloaded the table, Pavel and Dana's kind host asked if there was any way the driver could fit the Goia family's things on his truck as they needed to find a way to Andrews University. "I would if I had room," he said regretfully. "But I have another houseful of furniture belonging to a student here in Tennessee to still fit on this load."

A couple hours after the truck driver left he called back with some good news. The student from Tennessee had decided to postpone his move until the following semester. He was on his way back to load the Goias' things. Equally thrilling was the fact that the expenses of the trip had been paid by the two conferences sponsoring the students. The driver was offering to take their things free of charge. After loading their things the driver wanted to know where he should unload them when he got there. That was another problem. They still didn't have an apartment, so they decided that a storage unit was the only option. The driver began his trip north.

No more than an hour after the truck had rolled out of sight, the phone rang again. It was the housing department at Andrews University. An apartment had just become available. Quickly Pavel called the driver with their new address. In just two hours they had secured an all-expenses-paid move and an apartment. God had just moved mountains of impossibilities, and they were on their way to the next step of Pavel's pastoral education. In all his ways he had acknowledged God, and now he would experience the "desire of his heart."

As Pavel began his studies at the seminary, he and his family faced a host of new challenges. But certain that God had not brought them this far to leave them helplessly to their own resources, they were confident that God would continue to come through for them. Each time the Goia family watched God remove an impossible obstacle from their path, their faith grew. He came through in every emergency—although often at the last minute. Needed money would come just at the critical time of crisis, the amount owed and the amount received often matched to the penny.

Trusting completely in God's care, Pavel and Dana decided not to focus on their problems any longer, but instead to find others experiencing greater need than their own to encourage. When they miraculously received food, they shared it with those they knew to be in extreme need. Each time they shared with others, God replenished their supply. They were repeatedly reminded that it is more thrilling to be a channel for God's blessings than to be just a grateful recipient.

After watching God faithfully meet their needs, the Goia family began praising Him before seeing any evidence of His answer, and their joyful expressions were contagious. Many other struggling students were encouraged to face their problems by praising God rather than by pleading for His help. No doubt heaven smiled as it received the gratitude and praise flowing from the Goia family and those who shared their discovery.

Pavel found himself smiling as he contemplated God's many providences for him and his family since leaving Romania. Although he had taken a leave from the ministry to receive further training, his ministry had not ceased. In his new life as a student, God had used him to encourage countless other students and teachers along the way. They were his new "congregation."

With graduation from the seminary approaching, Pavel began to wonder where God's plan would lead him next. He reminded God that he meant what he had said to the customs officer in Romania. He would go wherever He wanted him to go when his education was complete. As he prayed to know God's will, his prayer as a 5-year-old under the apple tree in the churchyard came vividly back to mind. The verses in Jeremiah promised that he would speak for God. With his university education nearing an end, he determined that wherever the plan of providence led him, he would indeed be a spokesman for God.

Conclusion

Conclusion is perhaps an inappropriate word to use as an ending to the Pavel Goia story, as his prayer experiences continue each day. Just as the preceding stories from Pavel's earlier years represent only a small portion of the miracles he experienced, it is impossible to detail all those that have followed. His intimate friendship with God allows him to live each day in an atmosphere of light and grace. Pavel's life continues to exemplify the promise in God's Word found in Hebrews 11:6:

"He is a rewarder of them that diligently seek him."

One week after graduating from Andrews University, Pavel and Dana received a call from the Wisconsin Conference to serve as pastor. Feeling confident of God's leading, Pavel resumed his life of ministry in Wisconsin. He was called to a multichurch district much like the one he left in Romania, and with many of the same challenges. By his teaching and example he reminds his parishioners that problems find their solution in prayer. Several have followed his example and have discovered a life of miracles of their own.

Pavel has a passion to encourage others to share his experiences in prayer. He has been a featured seminar speaker on several continents. At times his seminars have begun with only a few hundred and then grown to thousands. DVD recordings of his presentations have circled the globe, with life-changing results for those who have chosen to put the principles he teaches into practice. Miracles have been noted in every place God's people have genuinely humbled their hearts in prayer. Often individual and corporate revivals have been the result. The words of promise Pavel heard his father read as a young boy in the churchyard continue to empower him:

"Everywhere I send you, you shall go, and all that I command you, you shall speak" (Jeremiah 1:7, NASB).

One MIRACLE After Another

God's prophetic word is still being fulfilled.

As an example of the miracles Pavel's congregation is presently experiencing while learning to walk by faith, a final testimony should be included.

For years the congregation Pavel was pastoring in Janesville, Wisconsin, had postponed building a new church. One impossible barrier after another had kept them from moving forward. As a result of many earnest seasons of prayer the members were impressed to move forward in spite of the remaining challenges. They were a small congregation with very limited resources, but they proceeded step by step, as the way opened before them.

It was nearing Thanksgiving by the time the foundation and lower level were in place and ready for the large steel I beams to be set as supports for the floor. Because of the long span from one side of the foundation to the other, very heavy beams were required to carry the load. Consequently a large industrial crane would be needed to set the heavy beams.

The building committee met and decided to have the I beams delivered even though they lacked the $4,500 crane fee. Frank, a member of the building committee and also a welder, volunteered to bring his cutting torch to the building site to cut the beams to length after they were delivered. It was a big project cutting the long row of heavy beams to length. Because of the thickness of the steel, the regulator pressure on the oxygen and acetylene cylinders had to be increased to make the cuts successfully. As the acetylene pressure gauge dropped to zero at the end of the last cut, the men were thankful there had been enough gas to finish the project. With the beams cut to length, they were ready for the crane to lift them into the concrete pockets along the foundation wall.

Since all the members of the building committee were available on Thanksgiving Day, they decided to meet in the morning at the building site. After they discussed the problem of the crane fee for setting the beams, one of the building committee members decided to call Pastor Goia. After listening to the account of their impossible situation, Pavel asked, "Have you prayed and given this problem to God?

"Of course we have," they assured him.

"You say you've prayed, but how have you prayed? If Elijah had prayed on Mount Carmel the way we pray today, he would still be waiting for rain. We have to pray in earnest for God's honor and glory. This is His church, and He is able to solve every problem we face. He has invited us to prove Him—to see Him at work. Let's pour out our hearts to God right now and watch what He will do," Pavel challenged.

Realizing their pastor was right, the men formed a prayer circle at the building site. With earnest hearts they began to pour out their need before God. When each of them had prayed, they didn't pause their petitions, but instead continued around the circle three or four times. The longer they prayed, the more faith and power surrounded their prayers.

As they were praying Lenny felt his cell phone begin to vibrate. Quickly he reached for his phone. The curiosity of the group of waiting men grew as they listened to one side of the phone conversation and studied the joyful expression blossoming on Lenny's face. As he thanked the caller and said goodbye, all were eager to know the details of the call that had interrupted their prayer.

Lenny turned to the others in excitement. "That was the crane operator we contacted to set the beams. He said there wasn't any way he could reduce his fee for his crane, but he would like to do something special for us today. He reminded me of his request when he was here last spring for us to pray for his son's safety while he was in the Army over in Iraq. Just this week his son returned home safe and sound. So he is offering to come for free today. He said that since it's a holiday and he wouldn't be working anyway, he wouldn't be losing any money. He's on his way over here right now," Lenny explained jubilantly.

Before moving from their prayer circle, the men offered their praise and thanksgiving to God for the miracle He had just worked for them. With thankful hearts the men moved into action to prepare for the crane's soon arrival.

Within a few minutes the crane was on site and positioned to set the beams. In less than an hour from the time the men had begun praying they watched the first beam lift from the ground and swing above the first set of pockets in the foundation. With men positioned on each side of the foundation wall they guided the beam as the crane operator lowered it to its wall pocket.

When the beam was lowered to the foundation it was discovered that it was two inches longer than the opening. After a few measurements it was apparent that the entire row of beams had been cut two inches longer than intended. They realized that this was more than just a slight delay, as Frank reminded them that he had used the very last of the acetylene and that the oxygen cylinder was just about empty when he had finished making the final cut a few days earlier. Since it was Thanksgiving Day, it would be impossible to replace the empty cylinders at the welding supply store.

Frank called everyone he could think of to borrow gas cylinders, but without success. So the men faced a very sober reality: If the beams could not be cut to the correct length, they would have no choice but to abandon the project until another day. They couldn't believe God would have answered their prayers in such a wonderful way just moments earlier for no reason. Certainly He wouldn't have impressed the crane operator to make such a generous donation just to have him return to his shop with the beams still waiting to be set. Once again the members called to update Pavel with the problem of the empty cylinders.

"You need to pray earnestly again. Empty cylinders are not a problem to God. He is able to provide the oxygen and acetylene as easily as He sent the crane you needed," he reminded them.

With the crane operator looking on, the men gathered for prayer once again. After they finished praying, one of the men suggested they try lighting the torch even though the gauges on the cylinders continued to register empty. Every eye was on Frank as he opened the valves on the torch. Frank reached eagerly for his striker to ignite the torch as the familiar hiss of escaping gas came from the tip on the torch. With the first spark the torch burst into flame.

Not knowing how long the flame would last, Frank quickly began to cut the first beam. When he was finished with the first beam, he moved to the next. Looking at the long line of beams waiting to be cut, the men held their breath, hoping the miracle gas would continue to flow long enough to finish the project.

Finally Frank reached the last beam with the torch still working perfectly. The excited men watched the last piece of steel sever from the beam and drop to the ground. To their amazement, the flame extinguished at the exact moment the piece of molten steel separated from the beam. It was time for a true Thanksgiving celebration. The Creator of the elements in nature had just created the gas needed to continue the construction of His house of worship.

While the beams were being set, it felt more like a praise and worship service than a construction site. Each of the men was eager to share the empty cylinder story with his family waiting at home, and it was clear that the crane operator would be telling the story at his home as well. Dumbfounded, he had never seen anything like this in his life. Every penny of his $4,500 donation was worth it just to watch God answer the prayers of this group of humble men desiring to advance His cause and honor His name.

Conclusion

The church building project continues to move forward, though many additional challenges have come. Little by little the members are learning that it makes a difference when we pray the way Elijah did on Mount Carmel.

Although we have come to the end of this abbreviated account of the experiences of a sincere man of prayer, you will probably agree that a conclusion to Pavel's prayers and God's interventions is not forthcoming. For each new challenge God continues to have a solution.

For many this will be not the conclusion but the beginning. For those who are no longer satisfied with the mere reading of thrilling experiences in the life of another, this is an opportunity to begin a whole new life of prayer! Why wait? God is inviting you to begin your own intimate walk with Him right now.

Friend, as you hold this book in your hand, you may be assured that Pavel has been praying for you. His deepest desire is not that you found his experiences with God enjoyable and stimulating, but rather that you have heard God's voice inviting you to step into the inner circle of His light and grace through prayer. Those responding to this special invitation may be assured that there awaits a "fullness of joy" intimacy with God never before imagined.

One day at a time God continues to bless Pavel and his family. He has always been faithful to the promise He made to him as a young man kneeling beside his bed: "If you put Me first, I will take care of you."

If you were to ask Pavel the reason God has been able to work so many miracles on his behalf, he would be the first to tell you that it isn't because God prefers him above others. Perhaps beside Pavel's name in the register of heaven it reads, "Because you prayed."

What would happen if each of us joined Pavel on our knees?

Pavel's Appeal

Have you ever asked yourself what plans God might have for you? In Jeremiah 29:11 God says:

"I know the plans that I have for you" (NASB).

God does have a plan for every single human being. And not just a general plan, but also plans for every day. Jesus would wake up early to pray, to find out God's plans for the day, and to receive strength to follow them constantly. David said in Psalms that before we are even born God knows all our days. For sure, He knows our needs, our strengths and weaknesses, sins and victories. He knows our problems before we even have them; moreover, He has a solution already prepared as well.

We pray and say, May Your will be done. But do we know His will? Often we pray and ask for forgiveness, for help in different situations, and for blessings, but how often do we ask Him for His presence, and for His plans? In Romans 8:32 Paul says that if God gave us Jesus, how will He not also give us *all* things *in* Jesus? That is, all needed things—*in* Jesus. When we have Jesus, when He is present and real in our lives, He has the power, the wisdom, the love, and the desire to give us all things, and all good things are truly in Him.

But shouldn't we desire Him more than His gifts? God asked ancient Israel to build a sanctuary so that He might dwell with them. Jesus came to be with us, and He was called Emmanuel, meaning "God with us." John says that eternal life is to know Him. In Psalm 63 David said that he wanted God's presence more than water—more than anything else. How different our lives could be if, instead of trying so hard to fix our problems, to fulfill all our needs, we would rather try to know God, to experience Him on a daily basis, to have His real and constant presence, and then to trust our needs to Him and His leading.

Again and again we pray for His help, then we try to do whatever we ask for ourselves, instead of waiting upon the Lord. We try to find the solution instead of doing what He says and following His solution. Shouldn't we trust that it is better to let Him take care of things than try to take care of them ourselves? Mostly all we pray for is ourselves and our needs, which places us at the center of our prayers and our lives, instead of placing Him in the center. When Israel sinned and Moses prayed for them, he didn't place Israel in the center, but rather God's name and glory. In effect Moses told God, "Yes, they have sinned and they deserve to die, but what are the nations going to say about You? Though they don't deserve it, please work for Your name and for Your glory." Paul the apostle reflected the same attitude: "What happens to me is not important. Whether I live or die doesn't matter. What matters is that I serve Him, that He is the goal and the center of my life. Lord, do with me whatever is for Your glory."

The more we are concerned with ourselves, trying to solve things, get things, and overcome things, the more we lose. But when we are concerned with His glory and His plans, giving up ourselves, then His presence in our lives brings peace, growth, victory, and the best solutions for our daily needs. Jesus says that whoever saves his life will lose it, and whoever loses his life for Him saves it. Remember, He says that *whatever* we ask God in His name, He will do it for us. He also says that if we have faith the same as a mustard seed, we can do anything, and that we will do greater things than He did.

Is Jesus exaggerating in these statements, or is there something wrong in our approach to prayer? Could it be that we don't really know how to pray, that we don't pray enough, or that we may have wrong priorities in prayer? Could it be that we talk much about God but don't really know Him and therefore experience His presence only sporadically in our lives? Could it be that we need Him much more than the things we request from Him?

We cannot even imagine how great God's plans are for us. Our imagination is poor when it comes to His power and love. We pray for small things, things we can usually do ourselves, often not daring to pray or think about great things, forgetting that He is the God of the impossible. Can it be that we limit God and His plans for us? God never changes; His power is unlimited, and His love is infinite. He wants to live with us, to work for us, to bless us, and to use us for His glory, to fulfill the plans He has for us.

What if, before starting each day, we would seek Him and His presence, ask for His plans for the day, and then make ourselves available? Can you envision what He can do in you and through you daily? The Bible says that if we seek Him with all our heart we will find Him, and in Him we will find power, peace, salvation, answers, victory, and joy unlimited.

And that may be just the beginning.